The Leadership Book

FT Prentice Hall
FINANCIAL TIMES

In an increasingly competitive world, we believe it's quality of thinking that gives you the edge – an idea that opens new doors, a technique that solves a problem, or an insight that simply makes sense of it all. The more you know, the smarter and faster you can go.

That's why we work with the best minds in business and finance to bring cutting-edge thinking and best learning practice to a global market.

Under a range of leading imprints, including *Financial Times Prentice Hall*, we create world-class print publications and electronic products bringing our readers knowledge, skills and understanding which can be applied whether studying or at work.

To find out more about Pearson Education publications, or tell us about the books you'd like to find, you can visit us at **www.pearsoned.co.uk**

PEARSON

The Leadership Book

Mark Anderson

**Financial Times
Prentice Hall
is an imprint of**

Harlow, England • London • New York • Boston • San Francisco • Toronto
Sydney • Tokyo • Singapore • Hong Kong • Seoul • Taipei • New Delhi
Cape Town • Madrid • Mexico City • Amsterdam • Munich • Paris • Milan

PEARSON EDUCATION LIMITED

Edinburgh Gate
Harlow CM20 2JE
Tel: +44 (0)1279 623623
Fax: +44 (0)1279 431059
Website: www.pearsoned.co.uk

First published in Great Britain in 2010

© Pearson Education 2010

The right of Mark Anderson to be identified as author of this work has been
asserted by him in accordance with the Copyright, Designs and Patents Act 1988.

Pearson Education is not responsible for the content of third party internet sites.

ISBN: 978-0-273-73204-4

British Library Cataloguing-in-Publication Data
A catalogue record for this book is available from the British Library.

Library of Congress Cataloging-in-Publication Data
Anderson, Mark, 1961-
  The leadership book / Mark Anderson. -- 1st ed.
    p. cm.
  Includes index.
  ISBN 978-0-273-73204-4 (pbk.)
  1. Leadership--Handbooks, manuals, etc. I. Title.
  HD57.7.A53 2010
  658.4'092--dc22
                            2010020891

10 9 8 7 6 5 4 3 2 1
14 13 12 11 10

Typeset in 9pt Stone Serif by 3
Printed and bound in Great Britain by Ashford Colour Press Ltd, Gosport, Hampshire

For Claire, Callum and Eloise

Contents

About the author

Mark Anderson is President of Global Strategy and Business Development for Pearson International. He first worked for Pearson in the period 1984–1997 in the UK and Hong Kong, latterly running a regional professional publishing and information business. For 10 years he worked in consumer goods and technology businesses, before rejoining Pearson in April 2007.

He was educated at Cambridge University and received an MBA from Ashridge Business School.

Acknowledgements

My first thanks are to my publishing team – to Richard Stagg for supporting the potential of this work, and to Liz Gooster and Martina O'Sullivan who have exemplified the very best that editors have to offer a writer. They have helped to make this a much better and more focused work than it would otherwise have been.

Above all else, I owe a debt of gratitude to every line manager I have ever had – I have learned a great deal from all of them. So thanks to Andrew MacLennan, Peter Warwick, Anthony Forbes-Watson, Rob Francis, Henry Reece, Graham Elton, Bachar El Zein, Linda Kennedy, Jim Glover, Jo O'Connor, Colin Babb, Nick Winks, Clive Hay-Smith and John Fallon. I also owe a great deal to Professor Laurence Handy who, as my Ashridge MBA Director of Studies, helped me and many others realise that they could be leaders.

But most of all, I want to thank my wife Claire for her support, and for teaching me more than she realises.

London, January 2010

Introduction

Purpose

Anyone picking up yet another book on the subject of leadership could be forgiven for wondering if there was any point in a new one given how much has been written on the subject over the last few years. My thoughts exactly – as I contemplated just why I wanted to write this book and how I was going to approach it.

My first exposure to business leadership came in the 1980s when I was recruited as a graduate trainee to work in the publishing industry for the organisation then known as Longman. I knew nothing about the world of work, nothing about publishing and nothing about 'running' anything. But I worked for someone who, while they consistently mocked everything related to 'management', represented something else very special – example and inspiration. And when I subsequently took an MBA at Ashridge, I came to realise that the qualities I admired so much in my line manager (who was, of course, sceptical about the entire concept of an MBA) were defined as 'leadership'.

After my MBA I was catapulted into running a video training business, which I think I did exquisitely badly. I assumed that all the theories learned during a management programme would be readily accepted by a willing and open-minded (and largely young) workforce – failing to realise that their overriding perception was that a 29-year-old with little experience of anything was an unattractive and, quite literally, incredible role model. Yet it taught me a lesson, and perhaps the one lesson that is the hardest to prepare for in an MBA programme – success in business depends entirely on people, and that there is no programme or course or degree that is a substitute for experience.

That very first line manager of mine was a natural leader, but my experience of experience has taught me that effective leadership skills can be acquired, nurtured and developed; that organisational structures which place a heavy emphasis on process and governance can suppress leadership instincts; and that being a successful leader is, more than anything else, reflected in day-to-day business behaviours.

Which is where this book came in. 'Leadership' is demonstrably a subject that is much written about, but it tends to be elusive. I was struck by how many current books on the subject analyse leadership either from a theoretical perspective, seeking to identify an abstract unifying theme that determines leadership, or from the vantage-point of a celebrated CEO, whose personal (usually said to be 'charismatic') successes are presented as a model for leadership action. While these very different approaches are clearly valid, they tend to avoid the harshest of harsh realities – that to be a leader, day-to-day in the teeth of tough and volatile circumstances, there is no time for theory and the experience doesn't *feel* theoretical, it feels all too real. However much we might aspire to be a Jack Welch or an Alan Sugar, most leaders are not CEOs of large multi-nationals and have to succeed without the trappings or profile or current, or likely, celebrity.

In an increasingly volatile business environment, there has never been a greater need for leaders who are able to marshal excellent performance, where leadership is not an end in itself but focuses on the optimisation of an organisation's major differentiation – their human capital. Demands on leadership are also complex; they follow no set pattern. The very challenges of global volatility that demand sustained leadership responses, also demand a leadership that is flexible, multi-faceted and, where necessary, international in perspective.

Perhaps one of the greatest challenges faced by a leader of any team is the necessity to confront a paradox – planned uncertainty. To deliver sustained leadership in the teeth of planned uncertainty requires not only a tenacity of purpose but also an attention to detail – an understanding that effective leadership lies not in grand gestures but in relentless engagement with people through every aspect of an organisation's quotidian existence. Effective leadership is both in the strategy and the detail, and *The Leadership Book* tries to demonstrate how.

The Leadership Book is not about rules for management – it *is* about suggesting ways to enhance performance through maximising the performance of people by respecting their inherent and unique value; it *is* about recognising that the effective leader must infuse such an approach across a wide range of activities.

How to use this book

The Leadership Book is organised into ten parts, which I believe represent the key areas that any leader of any team of any size will face on a day-to-day basis. Each part is sub-divided into specific action topics. All the individual action topics have been written entirely independently and I intend that you should dip into those that you feel are relevant to you at any point in your working life.

Each of the action topics has the following structure:

- a **headline description** including a leadership 'star rating' (see below);
- the **objective** – why you should take this subject seriously as a leader;
- the **context** – how the subject fits into the broader pattern of leadership issues;
- the **challenge** – why the subject can be difficult to deal with;
- **success** – how to deal with the issue effectively;
- **leader's measures of success** – three ways you can assess your progress;
- **pitfalls** – what to beware of;

■ a **leadership checklist** – a summary reminder of key strategies.

The final section focuses on leadership resources – human, technology and learning – on which you should plan to draw to increase your personal skills base.

The leadership 'star rating'

I have attempted to rank each action topic according to importance. While this inevitably involves a significant level of subjectivity, it is designed to provoke you into recognising that as a leader there really are some areas where you have to prioritise. Six topics have been labelled 'Leadership6' because I regard these as your *absolute* priorities.

one

Your leadership self

However much leadership is about the orchestration of the excellence of others, you are the starting point as *an individual* and must be aware that your words and actions set the tone for your business. Your behaviour – from your very first day in your organisation or team – is instrumental in defining the approach at all levels to the challenges and opportunities faced by your team; to the nature of relationships set with your suppliers and partners; to understanding and reacting to the marketplace; and to the attitudes to the management of people. But this behaviour of yours is also *scrutinised* – staff watch to see what boundaries you set, what expectations you have, and what behaviours you demand in return. And, more particularly, this process of forensic scrutiny is also on the lookout for consistency – consistency in your message, and the match of your words with your deeds.

Many team members are ambivalent. They want leadership and to be led – they crave the energising effect of being part of a team in pursuit of credible goals under the banner of an inspiring leader. But they are also likely to be sceptical – they will likely have been through processes of change before, and may well have seen leaders and goals come and go. So you must know that you face a sceptical audience, that you face a major task of *persuasion*; that you will meet willing followers as well as diehard recalcitrants and that, above all else, *all* your words and deeds must support your Vision (see pp. 45–52).

So to be an effective leader, you start with yourself – you ensure the strategic 'fit' of your own behaviour. You know that you have to set an example, and you make quite certain that the examples are set. You know that you are not only conveying a message, but that you *are* the message.

First days in the job

The first days as a leader in a new job, leading a new team, are critical: they set a tone, and convey an image that will define who you are and set expectations about what you want to achieve.

Frequency – one chance to get this right!
Key participants – all staff.
Leadership rating ****

Objective

As a leader of a team you can only function effectively by maximising the performance of your team. This in turn depends on how you strike and maintain relationships with your team members. Critically you must achieve, from the beginning, a fine balance between asserting clear directions and respecting the contributions of others.

Your first days in a new leadership role are the foundation of these relationships, and you must understand them as such. First encounters with new team members must therefore be thought through and planned. They are never casual.

Within these first days, as a new leader you send clear signals about how you will proceed – while you may wait to make decisions and changes, from the start you will nonetheless set a tone and create expectations.

*Your every move will be carefully watched, and you must be sure you convey exactly the **image** you want.*

Context

How a leader handles the first days in a new role – with such a strong emphasis on relationships – forms part of the strategy for an organisation's people, their roles and their value. Thus, during initial meetings with staff in a new organisation, you must indicate your attitude to:

- **the value of experience** – how an organisation regards the acquired value of accumulated experience;
- **the team as a 'community of knowledge'** – how an organisation identifies the premium attached to knowledge as a competitive advantage, and to the importance of continuing learning;
- **the role of the leader in the knowledge community** – how you respect learning, and yourself display the art of learning;
- **the power of listening** – you listen and respect the opinions of others;
- **the nature of decision-making** – how you balance your own decisiveness with the need to empower others to be decisive;
- **the power of principle** – how you set an example.

Above all, your role is to demonstrate the value of knowledge, and the knowledge value that all team members bring.

Challenge

Sometimes, when interviewed for new roles, leaders are asked:

- How will you manage your first days in the role?
- What specific strategies and actions will you adopt to manage your 'entry'?

If ever a couple of questions revealed more in what they don't say than in what they do, these are they. They betray an anxiety about introducing new blood, even though it may well have been the very reason for considering the leader's appointment at all!

This is the paradox you will face in the first days in a new leadership role. You will want to:

- respect the team in place, and be *seen* to be respectful and appreciative;
- impose your own mark of individuality.

Your challenge is not to allow concerns about 'rocking the boat' to undermine conveying your distinctive approach.

Success

First days can be enhanced immeasurably by careful planning. As a new leader, you should think about some key principles.

- **Information** – obtain as much information about your new team before entry, notably from organisation charts. It is worth the time and effort to request and study these because they will give you a broad contextual view of your new organisation. This alone may reveal some issues.
- **Planning** – plan the very first day in advance with the help of those who recruited you. The aim should be to meet or speak to direct reports immediately; and thereafter to meet all other staff working in the base office (if this is practical). Allow as much time for this as possible.
- **Dress** – remember that even dress will convey many messages. You should think about the style you are conveying – physical appearance can reveal as much as words.
- **Direct reports** – meet your direct reports as a group and set out your approach. This is not about conveying answers but setting the agenda for the way of working. Make it clear that you will be spending quality time not only with your direct reports, but with as many other staff you are responsible for as is practical. Tell the group something about yourself, your background and your experience – if conveyed sensitively, this helps to establish personal authenticity.
- **Staff meeting** – speak also, if appropriate, to the larger group of your staff. This is a crucial moment as it will set the

tone. You should not be afraid to take questions and make sure you give straight, non-evasive answers. If you don't know an answer, say so. Follow-up with an introductory e-mail to all staff.

■ **Stakeholders** – identify, in advance if possible, who the key stakeholders are. This should include key strategic partners, suppliers and customers. You should ensure that they are contacted early, and have plans laid out to meet them.

Leaders' measures of success

→ You met or spoke to all your direct reports on day one.

→ You addressed all staff in a meeting (if appropriate) on day one.

→ You identified your key stakeholders within week one.

Pitfalls

If 'first days' are vital in creating appropriate impressions, they also run the risk of creating poor impressions – which can take much longer to do away with. The main pitfalls are:

■ **a lack of planning** – if you give no thought to the 'entry' sequence of events – notably who needs to be seen and when – then the likely haphazard outcome risks alienating key staff.

■ **a 'know-it-all' approach** – no leader should ever convey the impression that they have all the answers. This risk can be high on starting as there may be a feeling of the need to justify the appointment with excessive statements of competence or intent. Any suggestion that the existing staff's experience is not valued can backfire. Modesty in the early days is a definite requirement!

■ **inappropriate decision-making** – any new leader may face unresolved decisions waiting to be made. Where possible, you should defer them so you are not forced into precipitate decisions based on inadequate evidence. Equally, you should not introduce change based on your own ideas without being seen to learn about your new role and to be seen to gather evidence.

Leaders' checklist

- Ensure that you receive as much relevant advance information about your new team as possible – organisation charts, budgets, business plans, recent appraisals, CVs.

- Plan day one with a specific, timed agenda – ensure that the timetable allows for any variation in staff start times.

- If possible, have the agenda announced to your team before you actually start – as part of your 'induction' process.

- For individual, team and staff meetings, plan their locations and any support you may need – refreshments, presentation equipment.

- Prepare notes in advance for all your key meetings to ensure that you don't miss any key messages – nerves may make this more likely than usual.

- Allow for time to have introductory one-to-one meetings (121s) with direct reports.

- Ensure that key stakeholders are identified and met or contacted.

Demeanour: setting the tone

'Demeanour' is the way an individual behaves in an organisation – it motivates and empowers staff to above-average performance.

Frequency – never-ending!
Key participants – all staff.
Leadership rating ***

Objective

The personal spark called leadership is frequently the difference between average and great performance. The key here is not simply what the leader should *do,* but what their team *wants* from them. This is demeanour – the way the leader behaves, day in, day out, across a range of issues and detail.

Make no mistake, in any team, in any organisation, the leader is watched every step of the way and all actions are interpreted – separately and cumulatively – as statements of intent about the team or the organisation itself. Often without realising it, through demeanour the leader will be sending signals about the organisation every bit as relevant as any mission, vision, set of values, business plan or objectives – and often more closely observed.

It's pretty obvious, but most staff know when they are in the presence of a leader rather than just a manager, and perhaps less obviously, in my judgement, they prefer it that way. There is no straightforward, concise definition of a leader, except we all tend to know when we are in the presence of one, and there's certainly more to it than the now-aged assumption that it's about doing things right rather than doing the right things. It's not simply about issuing orders, being liked or, contrastingly, making difficult and unpopular decisions – though it may be about all of these! It is also not about hierarchy or the trappings of hierarchy

– leadership is a characteristic that can be demonstrated in any role, in any function and at any time.

You must be aware that your **demeanour** *– the way you are seen to behave – is a hidden but essential part of maximising your performance.*

Context

Why do I say that organisations and staff crave this leadership demeanour? Most employees develop a bond with their organisations and teams which becomes close to dependency. Within that relationship they need a compass to manage their sense of followership. No one who commits at least one-third of their day to an organisation is likely to want to feel that it is in vain, that there is no guiding purpose. And that purpose needs embodiment at all levels in leaders – as expressed through their demeanour.

At this point two questions can be asked.

- Is effective leadership demeanour ever learned, or are the best leaders 'natural'?
- Does 'learned' leadership risk being seen as a performance, and therefore fake?

This is a huge behavioural subject outside this book's scope. Suffice it say that while some people are born with natural leadership behaviours, there is no doubt that learned experience can contribute to a leader's demeanour and effectiveness.

What you do in this regard is to know the importance of learning – and to learn from your own experience and by watching others.

Challenge

Being a 'manager' is a label many have desired in the workplace, and one which implies a degree of success. Often it means we take on responsibility for other people, a team, the team's activities, budgets and KPIs, as well as the corporate glare on that team's performance. It may also be a step-up associated with salary and benefits improvements. Labels in work are extremely important and we should never underestimate the prestige associated with progress along the manager–director route.

Equally nor should we ever underestimate the importance of 'management' in delivering performance. No organisation succeeds without attention to customers, innovation, process, delivery and its staff. Management has the most significant role in making these things happen. Most managers will succeed if they achieve three objectives – the deliverables of their team must be clear, the processes for delivery must be tried, tested and retested, and they have the right people in the right jobs.

The challenge to effective leadership demeanour is an excessive reliance on *management* rather than *leadership* behaviours. You must learn how management differs from leadership.

Managers	Leaders
■ Follow rules	■ Follow instincts
■ Focus on getting things done	■ Focus on getting the right things done
■ Side with safety	■ Side with risk
■ Focus on delivering today	■ Focus on articulating tomorrow

You meet this challenge by recognising that:

■ you are a leader (and don't be too modest to admit it);

■ leadership is not reserved for a hierarchical few;

■ leadership is about the tone of your behaviour, not a rule book to be followed.

Success

Does this mean that as a leader you are an actor? No, emphatically it does not because phoniness is always rumbled – but it does mean that, like an actor, you should be aware of the impact of your words and actions.

So what are the key aspects of leadership demeanour that teams look for?

- **Visibility** – be seen on a regular basis. Visibility represents involvement, commitment and contact and allows the 'you' in any leader to shine through.

- **Messaging** – convey regular and consistent messages. No leader is trusted who changes their tune!

- **Direction** – express a clear sense of where the organisation is going, why and how. No leader is worthy of the name who does not suggest to a team a direction of travel and clear, measureable goals.

- **Approachability** – be approachable on a one-to-one basis. Leaders who intimidate or are aloof make leadership remote and disempowering.

- **Listening** – listen to other people and absorb their views. You should openly respect the greater skills that all your staff will have in specialist areas.

- **Fairness** – deal with difficult situations fairly and with integrity. All leaders have tough decisions to make, and you will always be respected for the manner with which you deal with them.

- **Performance management** – be seen to reward success and tackle poor performance. Most team members respond in an environment where success is heralded and weak performance constructively highlighted.

- **Personal development** – be committed to personal development. Learning is never finished, and the best leaders and organisations never pigeonhole employees as 'beyond development'.

- **Innovation** – be open to challenge and new ideas. Teams innovate more when creative sparks are encouraged, and robust debate is welcomed.

- **Respect** – be wholly respectful of gender, ethnic and cultural differences. A diverse team reflects the world we live in, and a team whose membership is based on merit is a team in which opportunity drives innovation and success.

Pitfalls

One of the most significant risks to any leader is a lack of awareness of their impact on colleagues. Most critically your demeanour will be undermined by:

- **lack of contact with staff** – distancing simply limits the opportunity to make an impact;
- **lack of consistency in messaging** – this undermines the credibility of all messages, and especially strategic goals and objectives;
- **lack of fairness in decision-making** – decisions made without sensible consultation, or decisions applied inconsistently, will undermine a leader's integrity and credibility.

A leader has to stand out from the crowd. You won't if you are aloof, inconsistent and unreliable. At its worst, this potential masking of leadership creates a vacuum along with uncertainty and a lack of direction.

Leaders' checklist

- Be aware that you set a demeanour 'tone' from your first day – plan for it.

- Don't allow yourself to enter an organisation without a planned approach, and be sure that you are visible from day one onwards. It is vital to ensure that, as a leader, you are seen and not simply heard or heard of.

- Be consistent – set out ways of working and stick to them so that colleagues are clear about the culture in which they are working.

- Do not allow yourself to be buffeted by events, which will always include the unforeseen and unpleasant, and hold on to your basic tenets.

- Ensure that there is a predictability in approach, though not necessarily in outcome, so that colleagues have a clear view of what is expected of them.

- Be clear that the buck stops with you and that you are accountable, and not just the passive executor of others' ideas.

- Be clear that this means that you are accountable for tough decisions and that you will not shirk them. But, critically, never convey any sense that a leader's role is do others' jobs for them – on the contrary, it is to provide the circumstances in which they can flourish.

- Be honest – always say what you think and gain the trust that you are not manipulative.

- Be generous in communication – never assume you have communicated too much, and never stop. It is a golden rule that you are only believed if you convey the same messages repeatedly so that they are credible.

Leadership principles

Principles inform the action of effective leaders. They provide a framework of values based on respect which drive every aspect of a team's relationships and performance.

Frequency – never-ending.
Key participants – you're on your own on this one!
Leadership rating *****

Objective

Through principles, you as leader set a moral compass for your organisation and your colleagues – you chart your and your team's course by a guiding set of ethics that inform the way you relate to colleagues, partners and customers. These principles inform everything – from the organisation's strategy to your basic day-to-day interactions with colleagues.

The guiding philosophy here is that an organisation that is clearly and deeply rooted in a binding set of values will attract the best staff and best partners – and in the end forge superior relationships with customers.

Values are key to growing market share. Either directly – or through your brand – they express who and what you are.

Context

Any leader is a role model – this comes with the turf. Rather like a parent bringing up a child, sustained leadership actions are progressively embedded in a team or organisation. This rarely occurs immediately and is usually progressive and extended over a long period of time. But however subtle it may be, the cultural impact of leadership action is huge, because it is leaders who set out the standards of acceptable behaviour. The circumstances in many banks in the so-called 'credit crunch' give a perfect example – boards of directors leading through the example that significantly lowering risk thresholds is an acceptable (and indeed required) business behaviour.

Challenge

A likely response to charting a course based on principles is that, in the rough and tumble of running teams and organisations, sheer force of circumstance demands a more pragmatic approach. I would disagree – the leader's greatest single asset is *integrity*, which comes from being seen both to have and to exercise principles. You undermine it at your peril. Once devalued, once traded for easy options, it is a currency hard to restore; and if you are seen to be lacking integrity, you lose authority and credibility – and your team starts to follow through lip service and the demands of hierarchy, rather than through motivation.

Success

■ **Honesty** – leaders tell people how they see things without spin or distortion. This can be painful for all in the short term, as perhaps you deliver messages that are less than wholly positive or different from prevailing expectations. The benefit is that over time your judgement is trusted as a fair reflection of circumstances. This will in turn encourage others to appreciate the value of your straightforwardness. By contrast, a culture in which people say what they think others *want* to hear sows the seeds of its own failure.

■ **Respect** – you are seen at all times to respect others for who they are and what they say. You display an open-mindedness which aims to get the best from others by always assuming that everyone has a positive contribution to make irrespective of their role, background or character. The benefit you gain is to enable colleagues to flourish because they realise they matter.

- **Fairness** – you are seen to make decisions based on evidence and not on prejudice or assumption. You take all issues as they come without applying set or predetermined solutions, and are prepared to change your mind when evidence suggests you should. By demonstrating that challenges are evaluated on a fair basis, you will encourage colleagues to be open about problems and to have the confidence that these will be discussed in a constructive manner.

- **Clarity** – you say what you mean and mean what you say. You ensure that everyone in your team is clear about your Vision, strategy, goals, issues and actions; and that where there *is* ambiguity, this is because you are dealing with the ambiguous and are not using it as a means of avoiding decision-making or tough choices.

- **Openness** – along with being clear, you are sure (within any constraints you feel may reasonably apply) to tell your team the full picture as you see it. You want to avoid making colleagues feel that agendas are running from which they are excluded. Such openness on your part will be returned by a matching openness – creating a mutual trust that is the bedrock of teamwork.

- **Collegiality** – the effective leader doesn't sit in an ivory tower dispensing instructions and making decisions at a distance. You not only involve others in key decision-making, but also your whole team, where this is feasible within a framework of sensible time management. This will further engender mutual respect and help to avoid different parts of a team developing silo mentalities.

- **Decisiveness** – involving others in decision-making is not avoiding decision-making. To the contrary, it should facilitate it and it is vital that your team sees the benefit of decisiveness – not decisions made for their own sake (though sometimes any decision is better than none!) but in order to confront issues, analyse, decide and act.

- **Humility** – leaders don't have all the answers, they facilitate finding them. You make your team feel that they are all equally valuable, and that your leadership role is not about superior knowledge but superior facilitation. You remember to praise where praise is due, and never to take the credit for others' ideas or successes.

■ **Diversity** – you see the value of variety in your team and don't recruit in your own image or against stereotypes. You work with your HR team to understand the competencies demanded by your team's business environment – and also the mix of styles and experience that will give your team a competitive edge.

■ **Bravery** – perhaps the most important quality of all. You are sure, throughout your leadership tenure, that your team knows you are fully prepared to make decisions that court unpopularity or carry a substantial commercial risk. Such difficult decisions will seem all the more credible if made in the context of the other principles already discussed. They will inspire your team with the confidence that comes from doing the right things.

Leaders' measures of success

→ You use staff surveys (sometimes called 'climate surveys') to assess how employees feel about the culture of their organisation.

→ The diversity profile of your team is evaluated by an independent survey.

→ You encourage staff, via regular communication, to access and read the company code of conduct, employment, diversity and equal opportunities policies.

Pitfalls

Principles require determination, modesty and resilience, all of which are easily sacrificed.

■ **Determination** – principles will always be challenged, especially by those colleagues susceptible to easy ways out and 'quick wins'. Don't give in when you believe in what you stand for.

■ **Modesty** – principles are not to be trumpeted. Effective leaders do not stand up and tell their colleagues that their actions are based on principles – their actions speak for themselves, and their integrity is clear from their deeds and not their words.

■ **Resilience** – leaders can sometimes feel very isolated because through their actions they are under constant observation. This isolation can sometimes make the commitment to principles a stressful burden. So don't allow isolation to creep in – cultivate a network of peers you can consult and from whom you can draw support.

The moral for leaders is clear – don't give in to pressures to bend on principles.

Leaders' checklist

■ Be aware – as I observe elsewhere – that, like it or not, your colleagues and peers watch your every move, especially the actions and words through which you set the tone of the business. You are the moral compass – you have to know that as you lead, so others follow.

■ Know what your bottom lines are – know where and on what you would not compromise.

■ Remember not to parade principles but to lead by example.

■ Aim to have colleagues or, if possible, a mentor you can sound out on issues that are troubling you.

■ Learn to recognise the stress signs where your principles are under threat and when you are struggling to resolve the conflict.

Trusting your instincts

Instincts are good and they are necessary – leaders use them throughout the daily myriad of issues and decisions. Successful leaders trust their instincts as they trust others.

Frequency – it should grow on you.
Key participants – all your direct reports.
Leadership rating ***

Objective

How often have you had the experience of looking back at a decision made, or not made, against the 'advice' of your instinct and regretting that you had not been bolder? How often have you allowed factors that seemed more important than they really were at the time to deflect you from doing what you knew was the right thing to do? Most of us can probably confess to these feelings if we are honest – I am bound to say that many of my worst mistakes have occurred when I probably knew in my heart of hearts that I was taking the wrong course of action.

*To be a successful leader **enable your instinct** (some would call it intuition) so it is a key part of your decision-making toolkit. Let it be a companion whispering in your ear – and listen!*

Context

A CEO once said to me that the most important part of my job as a team leader (I was then at director level) was to be sure I had the right team – and that if this meant that I only needed to work half a week, then so be it! He was not wrong – as an effective leader you will realise that part of trusting your instincts is to be certain you have the right team in the right roles who are encouraged to make their own decisions. This is the first and most critical area where you must trust your instincts because your choice of team determines the outcome of so many future actions.

In addition, you will face occasions when staff come to you with an issue about which they are not clear over what course of action to take. The right approach here is not for you to think the answer through *for* them, but to facilitate their own thinking, teasing out if they actually know the answer but are unprepared to admit it or to commit to it. Trusting your instincts is thus also about building a legacy – demonstrating its importance and power.

In summary, the outcome is *empowerment* – doubtless an overused term but one which, in everyday effective leadership, really does happen. You really can see people learning to excel in following their judgement, and relish the liberation yourself of doing what you know to be right.

Challenge

There is an easy and possibly glib response to the value of instinct – that it is all a matter of experience. It can't be denied that there is always a 'first time' in taking leadership roles, and many of the approaches discussed in this book evolve as you learn how colleagues and staff respond to your styles of action. But the inevitable learning process that takes place can be accelerated if you recognise three critical traits.

- Like any leader you *do* have instincts and these are not only allowable in business but are vitally necessary. They are not to be sidelined as the preserve of entrepreneurs and are not out of place in the process-orientated corporate world.
- Trusting an instinct is not the same as being impulsive. An instinct is a deep-rooted 'gut' feeling for a course of action that may need to be tested out on colleagues or verified by some further analysis. An impulsive decision will be an emotional one based on a reaction to circumstances and is

not capable of analytical support. Your colleagues will very rapidly learn to discern the difference in you.

- It should not be your objective to be popular. A leader who follows their instincts will be undeterred from making unpopular decisions, but will have the convictional courage to stand by them. So try to prevent analysis from becoming an avoidance strategy!

Success

What is the benefit for the organisation or team in recognising and inculcating this approach? The gain is to develop a culture that is fast-moving and responsive with the following characteristics.

- **Common sense** – a value is placed on the common sense, ownership and accountability that most employees have to exercise in their daily family lives as children, partners or parents.
- **Experience** – respect is given to experience and insight, which are valued at least as equally as analysis.
- **Empowerment** – managers feel enabled to make decisions rather than have them checked in advance (subject to the authority limits that any organisation will require).
- **Decision-making** – a premium is placed on the quality and not the methodology of decision-making.
- **Speed** – decision-making becomes faster.
- **The individual** – decision-making becomes a tool for all staff individually and not always something that happens through consultation and meetings.

In the end 'trusting your instincts' is as much about trusting those of others as it is about trusting your own – get the right people, make the right decisions and empower them to make theirs!

> ### Leaders' measures of success
>
> Ask yourself – are issues nagging away that you are not confronting?
>
> Ask yourself – how many issues have you revisited because you were unhappy about the original decisions?
>
> You monitor how many conversations you have with your team where they are questioning their own decisions.

Pitfalls

Possibly the greatest danger in valuing instinct is that you allow it to override the requirement for more detailed analysis, to assume that instinct based on ever-increasing experience can always suffice. With greater experience comes greater facility in assessing how decisions should be made. A further risk is that excessive caution about instinct leads to a loss of entrepreneurial drive – and that this hesitancy pervades not only decision-making specifically but the broader attitudinal approach the leader needs to take to business.

There is a fine balance between instinct and caution, decisiveness and analysis. While it does get easier with time, the leader should be continuously aware that this is a balance that does *need* striking.

Leaders' checklist

■ Learn to recognise when you have instinctive feelings, and learn how to articulate them rather than bury them within avoidance processes.

■ Learn also to recognise the excessively emotional response – for example, that instantaneous e-mail response that should be sent to 'draft' – and to treat it for what it is.

■ Understand that after learning to be yourself, recruiting the right next line-of-staff is the biggest decision you will make.

■ Encourage, even train, your staff to recognise the value of their own instincts.

■ Review your decisions and assess how many are being made again because you doubted an original judgement.

Focusing on what matters

Effective leaders make sure they focus on actions which make a difference in reaching their team's goals.

Frequency – you need to remind yourself constantly.
Key participants – you and your direct reports.
Leadership rating ***

Objective

I once had the unbelievable experience, when managing a large multi-million pound project, of being challenged (by a corporate services division) about roaming charges for one Blackberry user in my staff. The hapless support executive who received my none-too-pleased response was doubtless only doing his job. He had been charged with reducing telephony costs, international Blackberry users seemed fair game, and the stated savings of £2 per 10 minutes calling-time was apparently worth his while. On the other hand, I was confronting project delays and cost overruns that, compared with roaming charges, were both material and relevant.

It is a now-established management mantra that success depends on doing the 'right things' rather than doing 'things right', and this remains a crucial part of a leader's armoury. It matters because what you do as a leader ultimately influences what your staff do, albeit sometimes imperceptibly. The organisations that are most successful are those most focused on the task at hand:

- having a clear segmentation of customers;
- understanding and delivering their needs;
- providing acceptable shareholder or stakeholder returns.

The risk that you face is that as your team or organisation grows and matures, it loses sight of these tasks, and acquires systems and processes that become an end in themselves.

*Your goal as a successful leader is unremitting **focus**.*

Context

Things that 'don't matter' can be said to fall in to two categories.

- **Things that never matter** – areas of activity that are purposeless in almost any organisation, and whose existence reveals deeper-seated organisational behaviour issues. Take, for example, the organisation that requires a written justification, signed by the divisional managing director, for a Blackberry to be issued to one of his directors. Sure there is need for a paper trail for both approval and asset management purposes – but a *written* justification? If any organisation trusts its managers so little in deciding whether to issue Blackberries or not, then it has the wrong managers. It should focus first on firing the managers rather than rationing the Blackberries!

- **Things that leaders *choose* don't matter** – the issues you decide do not matter. What is on this list will vary from time to time. How do you decide what is on the list? It depends above all else on your single-minded determination to focus all aspects of the business on explicit goals, and to refuse to be diverted to non-core activities. Take, for example, the organisation that has defined its key international markets to be the USA and Europe, but becomes aware of a substantial opportunity in Japan. The focused leader declines the unexpected opportunity and retains focus, rather than allowing the new opportunity to be pursued at the expense of the core goals, in a way which might suggest they were wrongly selected.

All leaders of all teams will always be presented with possible tasks, activities or opportunities that are peripheral to agreed strategic goals. They may indeed be tempting or interesting, but they must be rejected. Maintaining focus requires as much ruthlessness as risk-taking requires bravery.

Challenge

The business world we live in is one of rapid and extreme change – never more so than during the impacts of the 2008–9 'credit crunch' – and success requires a responsiveness, adaptability and decisiveness which may seem at odds with a constant and unrelenting focus. But this is to misunderstand the nature of focus.

Being focused is not about sticking to what you said you were going to do to your team simply because you said so – that is sheer stubbornness. A key element of focus, for example, may be sensitivity to customer requirements or achieving certain financial goals. Where customer demands change, or where financial targets come under threat, effective focus means taking actions that respond to changed circumstances.

If business environment circumstances change substantially, you should have enough focus on the implications for performance to be prepared to call for a strategic review of your team's direction, rather than perpetuate a set of strategic goals becoming increasingly out of date.

Success

Maintaining clear *focus* depends on:

- **strategy** – a clear strategic intent and Vision;
- **goals** – fixed and published goals;
- **structure** – an aligned organisation structure;
- **value** – insight into where the leader adds value;
- **advocacy** – constant repetition of strategy and goals.

With this in place you can not only articulate what matters, but be credible in doing so. It provides a framework for all future discussions on a wide range of topics, and sets a clear example to your colleagues of the way in which you expect success to be achieved. This will be helped by you being clear about what areas of activity you intend to leave to your team. Not only does this further emphasise your own focus, but through such delegation you empower your team in *their* own focus.

You can set for yourself a checklist of questions which you might usefully ask throughout your tenure to ensure you are on track.

- Am I clear about the organisation's Vision?
- Am I clear about the team's goals?
- Am I clear about my personal goals?
- How much time am I giving to issues not related to goals?
- Am I allowing my team to do *their* jobs?

A very effective supplement is for you to periodically list and review all your current outstanding actions (however important, however minor), mapping them against your checklist. This will give a clear ongoing indication about how far focus is being achieved or lost.

Leaders' measures of success

- Strategic objectives are linked to all team and personal objectives, and bonus plans.
- Team meeting agendas are linked to strategic objectives.
- You are achieving annual and strategic plan goals.

Pitfalls

It is all too easy to get drawn into what doesn't matter and you must be on constant guard against this risk. This is extremely likely if your team or organisation does not have clearly focused strategic goals, since all else follows from this framework. If you allow yourself to become unfocused, you will soon discover that:

■ your organisation becomes overloaded with non-critical tasks;

■ individuals in your team cannot describe their common purpose easily;

■ key financial and performance indicators will turn negative.

An unfocused organisation is commonly one that has the hallmarks of being extremely busy – the level of activity itself is a sign of inattention to a core purpose.

Leaders' checklist

■ Understand that no strategy is worth anything without a matching capability to implement it – and that a key part of implementation is focus.

■ Be prepared to focus on focus – talk and act focus, remind colleagues of focus and emphasise its importance.

■ Have the courage to pass opportunities by – however intrinsically attractive – when they risk defocusing the organisation.

■ Be humble enough to recognise that focus applies to you as well as everyone else and use the checklist and review process to ensure you remain focused.

■ Remember that your effectiveness as a leader is measured by outputs not inputs, and that you should not allow guilt feelings about focus to drive you to undertake additional tasks for their own sake.

Managing meetings

Meetings frequently dominate the working lives of leaders and their teams. How they are managed plays a key role in the development of organisation culture.

Frequency – the fewer the better!
Key participants – all staff.
Leadership rating **

Objective

Meetings are the primary way you communicate with your team members and they therefore play a critical role in:

- communicating strategy and goals;
- demonstrating principles and values;
- disseminating information;
- establishing personal relationships;
- determining the manner and mode of decision-making.

The effective leader understands that meetings are always about more than the subject of the meeting itself.

Plan your approach to all meetings for both the immediate (subject) and the underlying (leadership) agendas.

Context

In managing meetings, as in much else, you, the leader, set the tone. For example, if you work on a schedule of back-to-back meetings which become the main forums for decision-making then you set a tone of bureaucracy, stifling process, corporatism and not individualism – and worst of all a culture in which decision-making is collective and not independent. In turn, this may then create a culture of dependency on you – nothing of significance happens to which you are not a party (in a meeting).

You must also learn how to manage your time – not simply to fit everything in, but to ensure that you are allowing time for the right things. Meetings become a crucial instrument in this art of time management, since you have within your control the number and duration of meetings you run, and the number of others' meetings you choose to attend.

Challenge

Meetings present a leadership paradox – you will subscribe to the principle that communication is an essential lubricant for the machinery of business, but will also know that meetings are the bane of corporate existence for many in your team.

- How often do you meet people who complain that their business lives are dominated by meetings?
- How often do you make calls to receive the message that so-and-so 'is in a meeting' and feel frustrated?
- How often do you look at your own diary with the sinking feeling that at very best you will squeeze in the work you need to do *between* meetings?
- How often do you sit in meetings and feel that you should be elsewhere, that the meetings are overlong and poorly chaired?
- How often do you attend meetings whose outcome is either indecision or yet another long sequence of action points that will never be completed?

If you are successful you will be seen to be using meetings as a major instrument of communication, which staff welcome for their candour and effectiveness rather than resent for their irrelevance and time-wasting.

Success

Taking a stance on meetings is a central part of the stance you must take on corporate culture, entrepreneurship, decision-making and people development. It is part of the humility you need to cultivate – your role as leader is to create an environment in which great things happen, not in which you do all the great things. So have a clear meeting structure.

- **Regular staff meetings** – with all staff (face-to-face or via electronic media) setting out repeatedly a set of core strategic and operational messages. One lesson you will soon learn is that no messages are received or learned if they are not repeated (and thus given credibility). These meetings and messages set an overall context for actions.

- **Senior team meetings** – regular issues-based meetings with your senior team focusing on core strategic and operational issues, but no more than once a week.

- **Awaydays** – regular 'retreat' meetings with your senior team to create social bonds and to allow space for out-of-the-box thinking away from operational and day-to-day matters.

- **121s** – use regular one-to-one meetings with direct reports focusing on specific issues and progress made against objectives.

- **Non-meeting time** – where possible (apart from governance-related meetings, perhaps) you should have few other fixed meetings, if any. You focus your 'floating' diary time to be spent with current and potential partners, suppliers and, most of all, customers – or even just to be alone. This is when you do your most productive thinking about the future.

- **Agendas** – all meetings have clear agendas, timetables and monitored action items.

You must make it clear in what kinds of issues you expect to be involved – and that these will vary not only with the type of business, but also the stage of the development and business cycle the organisation is in. You should:

- explain how decisions on such issues are to be made;
- stress to your direct reports that they are accountable for decision-making within their own teams, and that you would prefer your involvement to be limited to second-line assistance in problem-solving – when you start attending your direct reports' meetings, you undermine their leadership and accountability;
- encourage all your direct reports to take a similar attitude so that, within clearly set limits, staff are empowered to make decisions and that meetings are best used to solve problems.

This is a discipline that is liberating, though it requires determination to implement. It frees up time, it focuses on issues, it takes responsibility for communication away from meetings per se, and will contribute to unleashing a positive wave of empowered, delegated, action-orientated responsibility.

Leaders' measures of success

→ You schedule necessary meetings – for direct reports one-to-one and your whole team – at least six months in advance.

→ You keep at least two hours a day clear of meetings for preparation and thinking time, with at least one day a week largely clear of regular meetings.

→ Your meetings start and finish on time.

Pitfalls

You have a golden opportunity in meetings that you chair to set an example. Equally you display the sloppiest of practices if you allow any or all of the following:

- meetings are not timetabled, but often held ad hoc;
- attendees are not strictly limited to those who can contribute but open to all-comers;
- meetings start late;

- meetings have no stated length that is adhered to, or have a given length that is rarely observed;
- discussion is unfocused and wanders from the issue at hand;
- actions are not noted, circulated and scheduled for follow-up.

It is important not to allow your organisation or team to become one in which the most frequent activity – meetings – is the least disciplined.

Leaders' checklist

- From the day you assume the leadership role, do not accept an inherited meetings structure. Focus on communicating directly to large numbers of people face-to-face wherever you can, and keep as much time as possible free for customers and thinking.

- Be persistent in advising your direct reports that you do not make decisions for them and expect them to be involved in problem-solving. Exhort them to create within their own teams a culture that decision-making is delegated and not centralised.

- Be dogged in the way you chair meetings (*see above*) to ensure that you establish a culture in which meetings have a purpose and are not an end in themselves.

- Refuse to attend meetings which you think are not for you, making it clear why you are doing so.

- Always try to be seen, and subtly take a 'meetings health-check'. Observe how many there are and how many people are attending them.

Time management

Time management is an essential element of an effective leader's armoury. Leadership is about people, and the nature and quality of time spent with them is at a premium.

Frequency – constant.
Key participants – direct reports.
Leadership rating ****

Objective

Time management is not an objective of effective leadership but an instrument. Above all else, leadership is about people and most of your leadership time will be taken up talking with colleagues formally or informally. Prioritisation and quality of interaction is therefore at a premium. So your challenge is to ensure that you understand the value of time and the role that time management plays.

First of all, you must recognise that once you have worked through your key leadership priorities:

- setting a clear Vision and strategy,
- implementing a supporting organisation structure,
- rigorously filling key posts in the structure with appropriate competences and
- setting up a complementary decision-making structure

... then you are nine-tenths of the way there. This is a short list but it involves decisions, and many leaders get them wrong – and if they get them wrong, they get the business wrong. So as leader, you must focus first on these and not on lesser details.

Once these four leadership priorities are understood (with a constant self-check mechanism in place) then **be ruthless** *about the allocation of your time.*

Context

How many of us have worked for or watched managers who send e-mails and make calls at all hours? Who are always the first in the office, or the last to leave, or both? Who convey the sense of constantly dashing from one appointment or meeting to the next? Who carry with them large bundles of papers, but have clearly not read them? These colleagues may perhaps have made the fundamental mistake in assuming that:

- leaders are judged by the hours they work;
- the most effective leaders are those who are best at juggling the heaviest workloads.

This is an essentially macho approach and is plain wrong – at the most basic level it confuses quality and quantity, substituting effect for effectiveness.

I have learned from bitter mistakes that effective time management cannot be achieved unless and until the leader realises what he or she 'is there for'. There is a fundamental that we could all do well to remember – the real difference an effective leader makes is limited to a few key decisions. This is why ex-Granada boss turned TV guru Gerry Robinson is oft-quoted as saying that he had to make only five or six key decisions a year.

Challenge

You learn to look for tell-tale signs that you are mismanaging your time:

- colleagues, staff or customers say that your Vision and strategy are unclear;
- you constantly ask yourself if your strategy is right;

- colleagues tell you that responsibilities are unclear in the current organisation structure;
- key colleagues' performance leaves you feeling uncomfortable or embarrassed;
- you start taking on tasks that key colleagues should be doing;
- low-level decisions are in your 'in-tray'.

You should immediately recognise that a common characteristic of these (by no means comprehensive) examples is that they take up time – thereby representing a loss of time effectiveness which is self-inflicted and avoidable.

You also look for what could be called 'superhero' tendencies in your work patterns. These are characteristics suggesting that you have convinced yourself that you can take on a near-infinite amount of work – for example:

- your work agenda is back-to-back meetings – there is little spare, reflective or personal time;
- you have regular work schedules that extend from 7 am to 6 pm plus dinners;
- you attend meetings without having read key documentation in advance;
- you are regularly late for meetings because your schedule is so tight that there is little or no scope for slippage;
- your meetings are constantly being rescheduled and/or cancelled because there are so many, and any changes have a major knock-on effect;
- you have a long list of outstanding tasks, which never gets shorter;
- key actions are not being taken because they require concentrated time and thought – you simply don't have the space for them.

When you realise that time doesn't happen *to* you, but is yours to *control*, time management becomes an art you can do rather than a challenge you fear.

Success

Suggested strategies for success in managing time include:

- **Time and strategic fit** – you will be approached by many possible business partners and suppliers for discussions, deals, contracts, acquisitions etc. The golden rule is not to have *any* meetings with anyone for the sake of it – you must think through whether the partners have any conceivable strategic fit. A short preliminary phone call first is a good filter.

- **Delegation** – delegate as many issues as possible to your team, and make sure they have clear authority limits and regard you as the decision-maker in the last and not the first instance.

- **Clear agendas** – wherever possible, try to ensure that your meetings have a clear agenda and, where they require a follow-up, that minutes are taken – so that meetings are structured and don't meander. A surprising amount of time is actually lost not because there are too many people-interactions in an organisation, but because they are allowed to last too long – and you will never find anyone who likes long meetings!

- **Value** – you must ask yourself, for every meeting or people-interaction, if you are adding value. You will be surprised to learn that if you follow your leadership priorities, you need to be involved much less than you think.

One final thought. There is a radical solution – a rethink of the basic approach to time. Days can be planned normally (major issues or emergencies excluded) to keep mornings wholly clear of scheduled activities. Instead, they can be clear for 'personal' work – e-mails, reports, reading, calls, preparation – and for colleagues just to drop in. In this scenario, afternoons are for planned meetings and interaction.

Leaders who take this on board may actually find that, if this is combined with a clear view of priorities, they have more time than they ever thought possible!

Pitfalls

If some or all of the following major 'snafus' happen, you should be hearing alarm bells:

- you arrive for meetings in the wrong place;
- you forget meetings altogether;
- you fall asleep in meetings;
- your assistant (if you have one) has a different calendar of meetings, even though you are both using Outlook;
- you are so unprepared for discussions that you have to be reminded what they are about.

If any of this strikes a chord *at all*, then you need to stand back and reappraise what you think you are there for.

Leaders' checklist

- Be clear about your role as a leader – it is actually limited to a small number of core priorities.

- Be ruthless about giving time to non-strategic issues.

- Focus on quality time with direct reports – better to see them less often for longer, rather than for snatched periods of time.

- Keep formal meetings structured and to the point – it is easy to waste time and no one likes unfocused and overlong meetings.

- Think about a radical approach – there is nothing wrong with having clear periods in your diary.

You and your boss

This is the most critical relationship in your business life – it determines your performance, your career development and your well-being.

Frequency – probably irregular meetings.
Key participants – just the two of you!
Leadership rating *****

Objective

Any sensible leader has a strategy for their line manager. It is about understanding, agreeing and managing expectations. What a boss will want is no different from what you will want from your own direct reports:

- clear and honest communication on agreed issues;
- early warnings of potential issues relating to performance, risk and reputation;
- regular information delivered to agreed timetables;
- delivery of agreed operational targets.

Your task with any line manager is to assess where the expectations and boundaries are in *each* of these areas – they will never be the same. For example, some line managers will demand regular written reports, some want regular verbal updates, some require communication only on an exception basis. Your task is to assess which it is, *not* to apply your own set of preferences.

*The key objective must be for you to **deliver** answers to your boss and not questions; to present remedies rather than issues – always to be seen as a problem-solver rather than a problem-maker. In this way, your boss will see you as a resource that assists, rather than a challenge to be contained.*

Context

Any line manager you encounter will always have their own set of issues of which you may not be fully aware:

- career aspirations;
- relationship with his or her own boss;
- performance targets;
- relationship with his or her peers and associated politics;
- competition for resources.

They will affect all relationships and judgements. So the sensible approach for you to take is to map out what you believe these issues are, and to plot your own support strategies alongside them. The alternative (myopic) approach – to see all issues outside your boss's context – runs the risk of alienating the very person you should be striving to support. If this sounds political, it is. And the more senior your line manager is, the more political it gets.

Challenge

You face your greatest challenge when you are finding it difficult to strike an effective relationship with your boss:

- you feel that you cannot easily anticipate your boss's requirements;
- whatever you do fails to win appreciation;
- you have the sense that your relationship lacks empathy.

In the end, of course, you are not paid to be friends with your staff or your boss and you will have to accept that on some occasions relationships will be better with some than others. A relationship based on trust can *only* emerge after a period of successful accomplishment, so you should ensure that:

- you *and* your boss are clear about the overall Vision and direction;
- you *learn* what kind and what frequency of communication

your boss likes (which might well be different from how they actually describe it);

- you think solutions rather than problems;
- you make sure that you are seen to put yourself out.

Success

The key to a successful relationship with your line manager is to have a clear and unambiguous understanding of expectations and to deliver them. The goal should not be to 'get on' – a successful interpersonal relationship is more likely to emerge from delivering objectives than to be a starting point.

You will be likely to succeed in your relationship with you boss on the following basis.

- **Objectives** – you ensure that you have a clear and agreed set of objectives.
- **Updates** – you regularly update your boss on progress against these objectives in the preferred manner.
- **Delivery** – you demonstrate (notably in relation to financial performance) that you are performance- and delivery-orientated and do not easily accept under-performance.
- **Solutions** – you raise problems as soon as you are aware of them, and demonstrate that you expect to be the source of solutions.
- **Advice** – you ask for help or advice when you know you need it.
- **Relationships** – you focus on managing internal and external relationships in a way that is to the credit of your boss (and does not generate negative feedback).
- **Priorities** – you adjust your various leadership strategies to ensure that you reflect your boss's own priorities and never allow other staff to see a lack of concordance between you.
- **Values** – you reflect your boss's values when dealing with other people.

What you are *not* is a proxy or carbon-copy – the most successful relationships are based on shared values and objectives delivered through complementary, but distinctive, styles and personalities.

Leaders' measures of success

→ Your boss gives you positive feedback.

→ Your boss gives you additional tasks and responsibilities.

→ Your boss asks you to stand in for him or her in meetings and discussions.

Pitfalls

If your relationship with your boss becomes impaired, it can take a considerable time to repair it. So the 'upward management' of this relationship is on your 'critical' to-do list. While this will always depend to an extent on the specific nature of your boss and the organisation, there are nonetheless some clear traps you should avoid:

- failing to take assertive action to deal with sales or cost performance;
- failing to complete specifically requested tasks;
- failing to communicate in the way your boss demonstrates, rather than says;
- failing to inform your boss of key performance or people issues early enough;
- failing to involve your boss in discussions with others – a key area of learning here is knowing where political sensitivities are; there will be colleagues your boss will always be especially sensitive about.

And these *are* all failures – it is your role to manage your boss as much as to be managed.

Leaders' checklist

- Position yourself as a problem-solver with a bias to solutions – always present a problem along with a possible solution.

- Understand the framework and constraints (often political) within which your boss operates – if needs be, write out a list of the issues you believe contextualise your boss's approach.

- See your primary role as delivering to expectations through attention to performance.

- Ensure in your leadership strategies that you reflect your boss's priorities and values.

two

Vision and strategy: the leadership mantra

Whether you lead a small team or an entire business organisation, you need to be certain that all your staff are clear *why they are there*, specifically:

- your organisation's 'reason for being' – your *Vision*;

- your plans for achieving your Vision – your *strategy*;

- your most important activities – your *priorities*.

This matters because in all organisations ultimate performance is the sum of all the specific actions taken by each team member, and performance will always be enhanced when everyone is working in the same direction with the same goals. This may sound obvious, but you must realise that Vision and strategy are not simply a series of statements included in business plans, or maybe in banners displayed across offices. If they mean anything, Vision and strategy must be translated into the activities of *all* teams in *all* functions. For this to happen, they must also be clearly explicable – Vision and strategy that can't be easily described are unlikely to win hearts and minds.

Your role as leader is instrumental. I have already described how as an individual you are closely *scrutinised* on your every action and word. To inculcate Vision and strategy in your team or organisation, you must turn this scrutiny round. You must develop what I call a 'leadership mantra' – a series of positioning statements about your organisation which you specifically repeat, and which you explicitly embed in many of your leadership actions. You have to be convinced that your Vision and strategy are understood, and are taken for what they are – the lifeblood of the organisation.

You must be sensitive to operating in the different economic, legal and cultural dynamics of a globalised trading environment. You must therefore specifically think through the ramifications of leading internationally, and how your Vision and strategy reflect the variety and complexity that is the globalised trading environment.

But wherever you lead your organisation, your communication approach is paramount – you must repeat elements of your Vision and strategy far more often than you think is necessary. Even if you feel that you are saying things too often, you aren't – you can never reiterate your goals too often!

You embed your delivery of Vision and strategy in a widely understood set of priorities, and you ensure that your and your team's actions are focused on success.

Setting and selling a Vision

'Vision' is a simple statement setting out why an organisation or team exists. It provides a framework for an organisation's values and actions. To be effective it has to be 'sold' – staff must be persuaded of its relevance to them.

Frequency – more often than you expect!
Key participants – all staff.
Leadership rating: Leadership6

Objective

As an effective leader you recognise that, as a living organism, your team or organisation needs to know what it stands for. You will understand that it needs an overarching sense of identity, which can be described in three elements.

- It needs to be able to define itself – to know and say what it stands for.
- It needs to understand where it is going.
- It needs to know how it will measure success.

This self-definition provides a framework for strategy, operational action and performance measurement. You have an unequivocal responsibility to state this Vision in terms that are simple and clearly intelligible – very often such a Vision can be expressed in a phrase or sentence.

The concept of a Vision is no less relevant for the leader of a team within a larger organisation – here the responsibility is to translate the overall organisation Vision into a Vision for your smaller unit.

Once 'set', the Vision must be 'sold' – repeated in all forms of communication with sufficient frequency and conviction to demonstrate that it really does underpin the organisation's daily activities.

*Your objective as leader is to ensure that **Vision is seen to matter**. You must create a Vision which is clear and motivating – and you must be seen to advocate it tirelessly.*

Context

Any leader's team will be organised to deliver *performance*. Organisation structure, job descriptions, annual objectives, personal development plans, annual bonus plans, specific incentives – these and more are formulated on the expectation of maximising performance, i.e. the intention being to recruit the best staff who will be suitably rewarded for meeting targets, working within a framework of clear accountability.

By providing a Vision, you offer a guiding statement that:

- individual team members find motivating;
- binds all performance actions together.

In this way, Vision creates something real – it becomes more than a series of words or aspirations. It is the common denominator that unites all staff in a common purpose of related actions.

You must have faith in the *value* of Vision since the Vision itself will probably not articulate specific performance measures. You must understand the sometimes intangible value of expressing generalised ambitions as a means of motivating and directing all staff.

Challenge

Too often there is a risk that too much attention is paid to creating a Vision, and too little to communicating it. Moreover, even less attention may be paid to 'selling' it. A Vision will only have an impact (i.e. underpin all performance actions) if it is seen and heard with a frequency that gives it credibility. It cannot be a statement prefacing annual business plans or reports, which are then filed away.

You must develop for your chosen Vision a communication strategy focused on selling it – i.e. the communication approach is based on enthusiastic advocacy rather than passive publication. So your Vision should be referred to regularly in:

- team or staff meetings;
- regular written updates to staff;
- team newsletters;
- the intranet and external website;
- internal and external presentations;
- press interviews (if applicable);
- 121s and informal conversations.

… and indeed any other opportunity! The key is *repetition* – you must never feel inhibited from a zealous and seemingly excessive restatement of the Vision. It will only be taken seriously if it is seen to be constant and ever-present – and not just another example of here-today gone-tomorrow management speak.

Success

Only time will tell whether the Vision you set for an organisation is achievable or not. In the near term, you will most likely lay the foundations for success if this most personal of endeavours is thoroughly stress-tested and planned.

An absolute prerequisite is that your Vision must be based on your beliefs and value-sets. It cannot be a view that you have borrowed, or be the creation of others to whom the visioning process was sub-contracted.

Key steps to success are:

- **'Vision' is personal** – the Vision *must* be based on your instincts even if discussed and 'sounded out' with others. I do not believe that successful visions are crafted by committee. Even if your Vision emerges from a team-based, collegiate review (perhaps in certain cases using the resources of outside consultants), the specific expression of the Vision must be of your own choosing.

- **The proposed Vision is tested** – it is worth trying out the Vision on a small group of trusted colleagues to test both their reaction to the overall proposition and also to the manner in which it is being articulated. The Vision is nothing if it is not clear, intelligible and repeatable.

- **The proposed Vision is simple** – ideally a straightforward phrase or sentence, not a long series of paragraphs.

- **Initial communication is planned** – how the Vision is communicated requires careful analysis, especially if there is a range of internal and external target groups for whom it is relevant. The larger the number of stakeholders involved, the more complex the planning – you must be sure that all stakeholders are communicated to at the right time and in the right sequence.

- **Ongoing communication is planned and intensive** – launching your Vision is just that; it's a start. The real test is to sustain its communication and dissemination over a long period of time, and plans must be laid to enable repetition. You must also drill yourself to take every opportunity, notably in face-to-face contacts, to reinforce key Vision messages.

- **Communication messages are refined** – there should be no assumption that just because communication was well-planned, it is incapable of improvement. If through the act of repetition better ways of communicating the key messages arise, then these should be embraced.

- **Annual and strategic plans are evaluated against the Vision** – the Vision should be much more than a mantra being communicated on a regular basis; it must also be a litmus test against which long-term and annual plans are evaluated.

Leaders' measures of success

→ The Vision exists – and there is a document describing it.

→ You refer to it often in meetings, presentations and 121s.

→ Staff can describe it (if asked during a staff 'climate survey') and it appears on your organisation intranet and website.

Pitfalls

Vision is weakened in four primary circumstances.

- **The Vision is too long or too complex** – quite simply, it isn't intelligible and is not easily explained.

- **The Vision is clearly at odds with prevailing business realities** – your primary responsibility is to orientate your team clearly towards achievable goals. If the Vision is distanced from these, your entire operation will lack credibility.

- **The leader fails to communicate the Vision regularly** – infrequency of communication will suggest that the Vision is a passing fad or being used to complete a management planning process.

- **You think the Vision isn't relevant to you** – if you convey the impression that the organisation's overall Vision isn't relevant to your smaller team, your strategic 'disloyalty' risks failing to align your team to the organisation's greater goals.

Leaders' checklist

- Ask yourself if the organisation or team you are responsible for has a Vision. Is it clear? Is it being communicated? Is it up to date?

- If the answer to any of these challenges is 'no', then initiate a process to develop a Vision.

- If you are creating a Vision, be sure that while you canvass the views of others, the nature and articulation of the Vision bears your personal imprint.

- Check the extent of the Vision – if it's too long, it will lack the effectiveness of simplicity and should be cut!

- Make sure that the Vision is referred to in all appropriate communication media, and that you personally oversee any communication plan.

- Train yourself to use all opportunities to reinforce key messages relating to the Vision.

Leading strategy

'Strategy' is a systematic plan designed to enable an organisation to meet its goals. You play a key role in shaping the strategy and, critically, keeping focus on it.

Frequency – annual reviews, ongoing reinforcement.
Key participants – your leadership team.
Leadership rating: Leadership6

Objective

If an organisation has set itself a clear Vision, it will also establish a series of goals. These are most likely to be a broad set of numeric objectives around sales, profits, cash and/or market share – in absolute terms, or measured by growth rate.

Managing the organisation on an integrated daily basis towards its goals demands a strategic plan that sets out key thematic activities. These activities will be the areas of focus to which all teams' individual plans contribute:

- allocation of resources;
- acquisitions and partnerships;
- organic investment;
- human resource development;
- management succession planning;
- external environment.

Since the strategic plan becomes a framework and benchmark for many future actions and decisions, as leader you must ensure that your organisation's strategy has three key characteristics:

- **clarity** – the strategy must be intelligible and easily repeatable, so that it can be communicated easily;

■ **realism** – the strategy must be grounded in the realities of the business environment in which the organisation operates;

■ **achievability** – the strategy must be attainable because anything seen to be unrealistic will lose credibility.

If strategic plans meet these criteria, staff will be motivated to support them, and you will be able to marshal all the practical and human resources at your disposal to meet your goals.

*Your objective as leader is to shape a strategy which is **deliverable** – you must motivate your staff through its clarity, realism and achievability.*

Context

Your organisation or team requires *direction* in order to be effective. This is not about you telling staff *what to do*, but *enabling* them to make their own decisions about the appropriateness and relevance of their actions.

Moreover, this *self*-direction is not simply about striving towards the overarching Vision, which in truth may sometimes seem distanced from daily activities and decision-making. It's also about delivering today's priorities. Strategy provides this direction – it enables focus on a hierarchy of targets, such as:

■ weekly, monthly, quarterly and annual goals;

■ related bonus and incentive plans;

■ choice of business partners;

■ prioritisation of acquisition targets;

■ prioritisation of new market entry plans.

You have a stark choice to make between effectiveness and ineffectiveness:

■ **effective strategic direction** – all your team's activities aligned to commonly understood goals;

■ **ineffective strategic direction** – priorities varying by team, by time and, at times, by whim.

Even in organisations famous for 'skunk works' (3M, and more recently Google – see also p. 205), time allotted to entrepreneurial stargazing is limited by tightly controlled overall priorities. The effective implementation of strategy requires a clear and ruthless insight that all activities must be aligned – otherwise the organisation will be undermined by *strategic drift*.

Challenge

Strategy can sometimes seem hard to hold onto when you are faced with the vicissitudes of a rapidly changing business environment – especially, for example, during the 2009–10 global recession which witnessed some unprecedented and rapid declines in business activity.

However, the most effective approach to such circumstances is to see strategy as a support and not a millstone. If the strategic view of market opportunity is correctly based then you will know whether (to take one example):

■ you are planning in a given business segment to harvest short-term sales and profits, and therefore have a (planned) exit strategy; or

■ you are investing in long-term value and have short-term financial improvement strategies, if needed.

Strategy will be all the more effective if it is designed to accommodate performance going to plan and *not* going to plan. The essence here is *management of risk* and *sensitivity to learning*:

■ **management of risk** – strategic plans should explicitly confront what actions might be required in the event of unexpected circumstances (e.g. a deviation of sales or profits greater than a target threshold);

■ **sensitivity to learning** – the organisation must have in place market 'antennae' which enable it to detect and react to changing circumstances, rather than pursue agreed strategies just because they are agreed strategies.

Strategic decisiveness does not preclude responsiveness – indeed, the most successful strategies are those that have built-in flexibility.

Success

Strategic planning will always follow specific guidelines and processes, which differ across organisations. However, successful leadership in strategy will be based on a core set of approaches, which are market- and people-orientated:

- **Staff involvement** – the team responsible for strategic planning should be clearly defined with specific accountabilities in a fixed timetable.

- **No boundaries set** – within the agreed Vision and goals of the organisation, a clear rule for strategic planning must be that no ideas are rejected out of hand just because they are new, or even were previously considered and rejected.

- **Market analysis and the unpredictable** – whether analysing product categories or geographies, strategising should include 'thinking the unthinkable'; no assumption should be made that current parameters will apply indefinitely.

- **Paradigm shifts** – a specific search should be made for paradigm shifts that fundamentally alter the terms of trade in the given business segment. If none appear likely then the search should be repeated again, and then again – they are there!

- **Geographic market entry** – if your organisation is considering entering a new geographical market, it should identify the potential visible and invisible barriers, and talk with experts in that market for verification; it should not make market assumptions at a distance.

- **Product market entry** – if the strategic plan includes the launch of new product categories, the strategic review process should consider not simply the opportunity as seen today, but also how the landscape may have changed by launch, especially driven by competitor reaction.

- **Competitor analysis** – a series of competitor SWOTs should be completed from an internal viewpoint and from *their* perspectives. A review process should attempt to gauge how competitors will respond to a new entrant's activities.

- **Supplier analysis** – suppliers should be reviewed not only for programmes of cost reduction (this should be a given) but also for your organisation's vulnerability to them; a reduced supplier base can be a fragile supplier base!

- **People resource and competence** – nothing in a strategic plan happens without people, and a key litmus test of the achievability of a strategic plan is the alignment of opportunity and people competence.

- **Value proposition** – clarity is essential whether competition is based on price or value. These Porterian distinctions remain as valid today as ever and drive key assumptions about all aspects of product, cost and marketing.

- **Brand and marketing execution** – these are not the preserve of consumer goods environments; how customers are aware of products and services is a key component of any strategic plan.

- **Technology and innovation** – it is not *whether* technology can transform your activities, but *how*.

- **Financial planning** – strategy must challenge the basis of all price and cost assumptions, especially those with which the organisation is most familiar; the complacency of familiarity represents the highest areas of opportunity and risk.

- **Contingency planning** – the strategy plan should have provision for the unexpected and for things to go wrong; it should not assume perfection in execution and market circumstances. A good tool is to stress-test financial projections with variances up to −25 per cent.

- **Development milestones** – strategy plans are not start–end processes, they have significant delivery stages. These should be treated as milestones that are measured in order to assess progress.

■ **Non-committed options** – development options should be retained in the strategy plan, representing potential additional growth drivers outside the plan's commitments.

Successful strategic planning is often facilitated by the leader's key team brainstorming in an 'awayday' setting away from the office and its distractions.

Leaders' measures of success

→ The rolling three-year strategy plan is reviewed annually.

→ Key ongoing strategic milestones are achieved.

→ Business sales growth exceeds the defined sector average – market share is increasing.

Pitfalls

Clearly it can be argued that not taking into account the criteria set out in the 'Success' section above represents the totality of strategic pitfalls. However, some are worth highlighting in particular.

■ **Partial strategising** – seeing strategy as essentially the creation of products and/or entry into markets without due focus on delivery, especially development, sales and marketing. The key risk here is underestimating the effort required to drive strategy forward.

■ **Overstrategising** – including in a strategic plan too many initiatives at once. Here the flaw is to assume that an opportunity is relevant because it exists, combined with a reluctance to make hard choices between opportunities.

■ **New market blindness** – underestimating the barriers (especially invisible ones) to market entry and making over-optimistic forecasts of sales growth.

■ **Business model blindness** – failing to understand the dynamics of a new business model, possibly including transferring to it (even subconsciously) assumptions relating to more familiar models.

- **Incorrect or inconsistent value proposition** – failing to crystallise whether competition is based on price or value, and mixing the two, leading to a confused competitive positioning.

- **Inattention to the importance of people** – believing that staff are an appendix or afterthought to successful delivery, rather than instrumental to it.

In strategy there is always a finer balance than seems evident between risk and recklessness, and between ambition and hubris. As a leader you have to learn to take necessary but manageable risk.

Leaders' checklist

- Remember that this is a team process – you lead to empower, not to decide for others.

- Agree to strategic goals that are clear, realistic and achievable.

- Never forget that strategic planning is multi-dimensional and requires commitment, as much to delivery as to entrepreneurship.

- Ensure that the profile of people is never diminished – your staff and their competence make the most important contributions to successful delivery.

- Avoid the pitfalls of trying to do too much or under-estimating the challenges associated with what you are committed to.

- Make your organisation a learning one – ensure that you have the 'antennae' which can detect and respond to market changes.

- Maintain focus at all times – don't allow yourself or your team to be diverted by interesting but peripheral activities.

International markets and strategy

Most leaders will have an international element to their responsibilities, whether through customers, partners or suppliers. You must learn to be international in thought and deed.

Frequency – intermittent.
Key participants – staff with international contact.
Leadership rating ***

Objective

You face what might be called the 'international development fallacy', the notion that increasing wealth and globalising habits can be combined in an international development strategy with nearly limitless possibilities to expand. Yet anyone who travels from Washington to St Petersburg to Kuala Lumpur to Sydney will know that tastes, practices and cultures remain resolutely varying.

The lesson is that in an internationalised market customers want products and experiences that often link them emotionally and practically to a global culture, while retaining key aspects of the identity that make them who they are – customers want the benefits of scale while retaining the values of their community. This is an ambiguity (and opportunity) that requires a leadership-led *learning* approach.

No leader can do this learning for a team – you can only convey some key messages through words and actions that demonstrate that the learning must happen.

- Business visions, strategies and plans should have clear definitions of market opportunity so that market learning is focused.

- You should be seen to visit key markets regularly to demonstrate that real learning is done there and not in the familiar perspective of HQ.

- You should constantly reiterate the significance of the value of difference and indicate, for example, that terms we often use (out of familiarity and convenience) to bring people and markets together (like 'Europe' and 'Asia') contain at least as much difference as they do similarity.

*A key international leadership objective is to develop a culture in which as much emphasis is placed on future **learning** as on current knowledge.*

Context

Your team is likely to meet an international dimension in its activities in one of four ways – via customers, via suppliers, via partners or through internal operations in other countries. This will immediately present the challenge of dealing with different business cultures, and fundamentally you have a choice of only two approaches:

- you display the mindset that the 'home' approach to doing business applies everywhere;

- you believe that successful international relationships are based on a respect for and an acceptance of difference.

This is the core cultural value you must demonstrate when it comes to international transactions. It can be argued that this is a matter of choice, especially if the business has a dominant domestic market. But there can be few businesses that are entirely domestic – even if the focus is on domestic customers, an organisation should be investigating both ways of reducing its cost base by using international suppliers and also the likelihood of new entrants to its market from other countries.

The bottom line is that in a globalised economy this should no longer be a choice to make. But it *is* a real choice because you will still meet colleagues, whether through inexperience or sheer arrogance, who believe that a key element of doing international business is the application elsewhere of their chosen domestic business model. They also believe that it is not only the specific product or service that they are delivering in other markets but also their culture, their assumptions and, above all else, their *achievements*. They assume that whatever it was they think they did to be successful at home, will work elsewhere.

Challenge

Positioning your team or organisation internationally, you should always put first *what you do not know*. Much debate about international business can focus on the strategic business model.

- **Export** – an organisation finds markets for a standard product with no change to tailor it to local markets; making limited investment in local market structures.
- **International** – investment locally in markets already developed via export. This will include a limited refining or developing of products to suit local tastes.
- **Global** – the delivery of products across many countries, with a standard core tailored to specific market requirements, supported by local company structures, where globalisation has created standardised demand (e.g. computer software).
- **'Glocal' or globally local** – the reverse of 'international', the organisation is positioned effectively as a local business blending global resources, products and competencies with products specific to the local market.

This challenge of choice between these models, or changing from one to another, is a legitimate consideration. Your organisation will already be acting on the assumptions underlying at least one of these models. Yet implementing or operating one of these models assumes a level of knowledge that should not be taken for granted, a certainty about international market conditions that should never go unchallenged. What you should do therefore is be *contrarian*:

- challenge the way international markets are addressed;
- challenge the way your team thinks about international markets;
- provoke ongoing debate about international market dynamics.

Being contrarian is vital – if ever an organisation needs to develop its intellectual capital it is in the international arena, where it must come to terms with a sometimes dazzling array of economic, social, political, cultural, legal and competitive factors. In this quest for knowledge, you are the *intellectual* leader – not in asserting a model, not in asserting knowledge, but in asserting ignorance. It is this assumption of ignorance that can make a sophisticated organisation the intellectual leader. Such is the constant contrarian challenge to the status quo, it accepts that a position of complete understanding is never reached.

Success

The combination of asserting the value of difference, and a contrarian approach to understanding, is volatile and powerful and potentially hugely insightful. It enables you to instil in your team an approach to international business development based not on transactional models (albeit these ultimately have to be implemented for practical and operational reasons), but instead on an overriding sensitivity to international diversity and change. This is as demanding a task as any leader faces, not least because the increasingly and obviously globalised nature of the twenty-first century economy, with many shared products and tastes, can lure business teams into assumptions that convergence of customer behaviour is inevitable. So it falls to you to:

- **prioritise** – always ensure that your international priorities are clear and manageable, and are not seduced by the scale of opportunity into ambitions which cannot be supported by resources;

- **learn** – constantly remind your team that everyone always knows less about their international markets than they think they do;

- **take time** – never cease investing personal time in key markets, you lead by setting the example that improved understanding comes from engagement;

- **think international** – never assume that what works in the home domestic market is right for any other country, it's never as simple as that!

- **be humble** – always expect to be wrong and to have to change tack.

Leaders' measures of success

International sales growth.

Target market share was achieved in international markets.

New markets were entered in the previous one, three and five years against plan.

Pitfalls

I have already described the risks associated with entry into markets based on domestic market assumptions. These are obvious risks, but no less significant are the risks arising from a committed but possibly overzealous advocate of international market development.

- **Paying lip-service to international development** – where commitment and even learning are not matched by the commitment of resource; half-hearted investment in a targeted market is probably worse than none.

- **Knowledge is superficial** – where inadequate research has been undertaken and visible and invisible entry barriers are underestimated.

- **Lack of commitment to local experience** – where commitment is undermined by a lack of investment in senior enough and empowered local staff who can bring to bear their specific market knowledge; where learning is subservient to a residual expat management culture.

■ **Operating in too many markets** – where enthusiasm about opportunity leads to 'overreach', and an organisation tries to undertake too many activities at once spreading its resources thinly over too many geographic locations.

Leaders' checklist

■ Focus on learning – you must ensure that your staff who have international responsibility know that learning about international markets never ends.

■ Be clear that it is flawed to assume that what works in one environment necessarily represents best practice everywhere.

■ Lead by example and visit key markets regularly to demonstrate that the best learning about a market takes place in the market itself.

■ Stagger your investment in new markets to ensure that you approach each thoroughly and effectively, rather than tackling too many at once.

■ Prioritise investment in local staff with local knowledge.

■ Watch your own and your organisation's language and adapt it with the times – say 'Asia Pacific' rather than 'the Far East', for example.

Leadership priorities

A leader can easily be diverted from priorities – to be focused on them, you must know what they are!

Frequency – constant!
Key participants – direct reports.
Leadership rating: Leadership6

Objective

The leader of a team will face what will sometimes seem like a constant challenge to priorities – the ebb and flow of day-to-day issues, dealing with the unexpected, organising yourself to deal with planned meetings and reports, keeping on top of e-mail and spending quality time with your direct reports and key partners and customers.

The major risk to you, and to your performance, is that you allow yourself to be buffeted by events, and to feel – and even to be seen – to be responding to whatever happens next. The sense – if it can be admitted – of being out of control in this way is an unpleasant one, and one you need to learn to recognise. The tactical solution is always to review time management strategies. However, no approach to time management is really worth it, or is going to be ultimately effective, if you are not clear what you are managing your time *for*.

*You must have a **framework of practical priorities** to inform choices about how to invest your time and energy.*

Context

Day-to-day priorities are the most practical expression of the implementation of your Vision and strategy. It is at this point that your view of yourself intersects with the way you define and manage your team. So in prioritising, you combine:

- a distillation of your organisation's **Vision**;
- an insistent focus on **goals**;
- a constant reminder of core **strategies**;
- your **leadership** persona;
- the messages you use to lead and motivate your **team**;
- your attention to **performance** delivery.

This remains an ever-present issue – ensuring that these factors remain in balance and that you are not buffeted by events into well-meant but marginal activities.

Challenge

A legitimate challenge is how *leadership* relates to *management* and the extent to which you as a leader regard 'management' as part of your responsibilities.

- **Being a manager** is about role, hierarchy and process. Organisations employ positions which, in their very definitions, are said to include 'management'; which have a place in the structure that are recognised as managerial within the organisation's formal or informal hierarchical code; and which demand participation in specific HR processes. A manager may or may not have direct line management responsibility for others. Most colleagues will know who the 'managers' are and will recognise that good managers execute job-specific and organisational tasks effectively – for example, they organise appraisals on time and record their outcomes faithfully.

- **Being a leader** demands unerring focus on delivery through people – by definition, the *leader* needs the *led*. Leaders have a clear view of what they want to achieve and how – by making a small number of key decisions about the organisation's structure and its staff; and by relentlessly and unerringly informing their approach to everyday business activities with the view that all staff are capable of superior performance when properly motivated.

In essence:

- being a manager is about how you see yourself;
- being a leader is about how you see others.

You will need to be an effective manager to deal with necessary corporate and team processes and governance. But in bringing together the Vision, goals and strategy you are a leader first and a manager second.

Success

As a successful leader you understand that there are six key practical priorities which inform your use of time.

- **Developing and communicating a clear Vision and strategy** – your team will need a clear sense of purpose. They want a game plan. You continuously advocate, promote and refer to the core Vision and strategy. Credibility is maximised by continual reinforcement.

- **Implementing a supporting organisation structure** – you assess your team or organisation's structure to ensure that it has a focus on the competencies needed to deliver the goals. Your primary objective is to put in place a structure that affords your team the greatest chance of success. This may actually involve an overall reduction in activities – many a team has underperformed because a mistakenly ambitious belief in the limitlessness of its capabilities became a lack of attention to what really mattered.

- **Rigorously filling key posts in the structure with appropriate competences and values** – 'fit the people to the jobs, not the jobs to the people' I was once told, and how true this is, and how easy it is not to do it! You *don't* want clones of yourself – to the contrary you will welcome a team with members contributing distinctive personalities. You *do* want them to share your values and be likely to take your stance on issues. You seek not to create uniformity, but a shared identity of purpose. If you cannot put trust in your team at this level, you will be unable to delegate and empower effectively.

- **Establishing a complementary decision-making structure** – your team must know how decisions are made, who needs to be involved and what they themselves have the power to decide. This is a fundamental crutch both to personal empowerment and also team-building. The decisions you make, and the way you make them, significantly characterise the type of team you are creating, and each individual's sense of identity within it.

- **Continuously monitoring performance** – you review on a weekly, monthly and quarterly basis the financial, operational and service milestones agreed for your business. These milestones and the actual performance against them are transparent and published.

- **Relentlessly motivating** – you do everything you can to make your team feel respected and valued, and that they can achieve their goals.

Leaders' measures of success

→ Progress against milestones as set out in a strategic plan.

→ There is a low backlog of open issues awaiting decisions – perhaps as tracked in a weekly management meeting.

→ Weekly, quarterly and annual targets are achieved and exceeded.

Pitfalls

There are generally few risks in remaining focused on agreed tasks. However, every leader needs to beware of falling into two major traps.

- **Becoming blinkered to changes in the strategic landscape** – being so focused on delivery against agreed goals and targets that you overlook the way the market (and therefore targets) have shifted.

- **Disregarding important but non-priority issues** – being so orientated to key strategic tasks that you overlook issues that need managerial attention but seem remote, and which if left unresolved may actually cause problems.

This can be an extraordinarily difficult balancing act. Over time, and with experience, the best leaders develop extremely sensitive antennae to pick up warning signals and prevent themselves from falling into these two traps.

Leaders' checklist

- Constantly remind yourself of the six leadership priorities.

- Be prepared to articulate and reinforce your Vision and strategy more frequently than you think is necessary.

- Constantly review your organisation's structure to ensure that it delivers focus on business opportunities.

- Constantly review the appropriateness of your team and its performance to your goals.

- Regularly assess if your decision-making structures are enabling the decisions you need to make and with the timeliness that is required.

- Solicit feedback about your own performance – check that your team feels it is being empowered and motivated to achieve its best.

three

Your leadership team

Your leadership team is your immediate group of direct reports. You will spend more waking hours with them individually and collectively during workdays than any other group in your life, including your family. As a group they will therefore significantly colour your whole life – your work experience, your effectiveness, your organisation's or team's success, and indeed your own sense of well-being.

Most leaders inherit a team when they assume a role, and this means not only the team members but also their group and personal behaviours. You must set about implementing your own modus operandi for a team which has become your own.

You need to set about establishing:

- a clear set of expectations for performance;

- standards of individual and group behaviour;

- personal relationships with each team member;

- the organisation and team structure you want;

- whether or not the individuals you have fit the roles you need;

- whether or not new team members need to be recruited.

The relationship you have with your team members is a paradox. With the individuals to whom you commit so much time, you cannot develop a close personal relationship – you have instead a demanding and sometimes intensive work-driven relationship that retains distinct barriers. You have friendship, but it is a work friendship. You share many emotions, many challenges, many highs and lows – but in the end you leave the office behind and go home. And in some sense, home is never far away, since you as leader must always retain barriers. These are essential to maintaining focus – cross them and the intrusion of the personal undermines your ability to manage your team's performance.

So this most personal of leadership roles can also be the most lonely.

Defining your leadership team

Your leadership team is your key group of working colleagues, with whom you spend most time – their definition and selection is one of your main priorities.

Frequency – periodic, but more often than you expect.
Key participants – you're largely on your own on this one.
Leadership rating: Leadership6

Objective

Let's start by defining what a 'leadership team' is *not* about. It is not about:

- selecting the individuals who will report to the team or organisation leader;
- determining who will attend management meetings;
- deciding who will have job titles implying a specific level of responsibility within a hierarchy.

All of these may be outcomes. However, defining a team starts with your customers and your team's interface with them. You may have a responsibility for an entire business covering all functions. You may, alternatively, be responsible solely for customer service. Your customers may be external, they may be internal. Either way your first task is to analyse these points of customer interface, and assess whether your structure reflects your customers' needs and priorities, or not. In so doing you also consider if these needs are appropriately matched by necessary competencies and commitment of resources.

This approach will generate a review of your organisation structure. Irrespective of whether it needs changing, it should *always* be reviewed so you feel ownership of it. Only then, and only then, should key leadership roles be defined (or redefined).

The last stage is assessing who fits each role, and whether this process of appropriate 'fit' is going to involve any changes to existing personnel or not.

It is an absolute prerequisite that the structure meets the needs of the organisation's marketplace, and that you fit people to jobs and not jobs to people.

*Your goal is to ensure you have an **appropriate customer-facing structure** with your direct reports fitting their jobs, not jobs tailored to suit them.*

Context

Several other factors will affect the view or review of your leadership team.

- **Broader questions about the Vision, strategy and goals** – are these likely to require a structural review?
- **Planned and exceptional timetables for strategic reviews** – how do these relate to your timetable for looking at your team?
- **Current business performance** – does this suggest a non-strategic team change?
- **Immediate evaluation of the staff you have inherited** – does this raise any immediate concerns?
- **The extent to which wide-ranging change programmes are required** – do these impact on the structure and the composition of the leadership team?

Managing and balancing these factors requires considerable pragmatism. You will have a team in place from day one and the definition and redefinition of this team must be flexible and ongoing. It is unlikely to be static.

Challenge

If the leadership team is unlikely to be static then it will have some element of built-in uncertainty. This risk here is that this could be destabilising – team members will be more concerned with defending their existing positions than focusing on the future.

You must be determined and consistent. From the outset you should state plainly and unambiguously that:

- a leadership team is never fixed;
- it will be continually reviewed in the light of strategy and performance;
- roles will be defined by market needs;
- change is normal rather than exceptional.

This is perhaps the greatest challenge of all that you set your team – namely that they simultaneously represent both stability and change, both continuity and adaptation, both authority and fragility.

To succeed, an organisation must incorporate change as a normal process – this applies no less to the formation, maintenance and reformation of your leadership team.

Success

The watchword for success in defining a leadership team is *pragmatism* – acceptance that it is always a work in progress, always susceptible to the need for change. To maximise success you will:

- **put strategy first** – understand that organisation structure and the consequential leadership team are instruments of strategy, not an end in themselves;
- **put jobs before people** – design the structure and team to be driven by success, not by the people you happen to have;
- **be uninhibited** – in changing the composition and members of the team you inherit;
- **maintain a personal distance** – remember that the ability to make tough decisions about structure and teams is compromised by over-friendly relationships;

- **be flexible** – expect that the structure and members of a leadership team will change repeatedly as the business constantly adjusts to market circumstances;

- **take advice** – from those who have organisation-design experience, for example your HR professional;

- **sound out your line manager** – keep them in the loop so there are no surprises.

At all times the leadership team is your team, your creation. It is yours to mould and refashion. With that control comes ultimate accountability.

Leaders' measures of success

→ Your leadership team structure and composition is reviewed within three months of your assuming a new leadership role.

→ Your leadership team structure is reviewed within the annual strategic planning processes.

→ You discuss the appropriateness of your team structure and its members on a fixed basis with your boss – as a minimum every six months.

Pitfalls

You must be especially aware:

- **not to decouple structure from strategy** – this risks undermining the credibility of strategy and leads to uncertainty about focus;

- **not to review structure virtually constantly** – maintaining a structure and team can be comfortable, but if they are kept too long they can become an operational and performance drag;

- **not to recognise where structure itself can contribute to poor performance** – poor structure design and poor job recruitment can themselves lead to weak performance, which may otherwise be mistakenly blamed on other factors.

I have indicated several times that leaders must not design structures to suit their team members. More risky, potentially egregious, is to make new appointments which are clearly not merit-based. This might include appointing colleagues with whom you have worked previously. To some extent this is understandable – leaders frequently seek an anchor in such 'repeat' colleagues because they bring a relationship of trust which can otherwise takes years to develop. But you should beware of appearing to give to these known colleagues preferential roles or access – this may be divisive and leave you open to challenges concerning integrity.

Leaders' checklist

- Remember that your team is not an end in itself – its composition follows a careful review of your strategic direction and structural requirements.

- Ensure that you design your structure first and identify relevant jobs second – don't make a structure to fit jobs.

- Constantly remind your leadership team that you are an agent of change and that nothing is sacrosanct – including the team structure of which they are a part.

- Learn to identify when repeated problems are caused by an ineffective structure or team membership rather than by process factors.

Managing your leadership team

Your defined leadership team is no different from any other team – it needs rules of engagement to operate effectively.

Frequency – ongoing, especially weekly meetings.
Key participants – direct reports.
Leadership rating **

Objective

Your leadership team is critical in a number of important respects.

- You depend on each team member to represent core values, and explain core actions, to his or her own team.

- You depend on each team member honestly to raise issues of importance that you need to be aware of.

- The senior leadership team is an important support mechanism for you in maintaining credibility with key constituencies – for example partners, suppliers and especially your own boss!

- Who you choose to have in you own direct team, and how you are seen to manage them, sends important signals to the organisation as a whole about your motivation, commitment, demeanour and values.

- The cohesiveness of the senior leadership team through the consistency of its messages plays a key role in under-pinning the credibility of an organisation's Vision and strategy.

- The modus operandi of the team – how it meets, interacts, displays itself – sets a tone and standards that the organisation will tend to follow, even if unknowingly.

■ You need to be aware that, in some respects, each of your senior leadership team is a personal ambassador and that their actions will reflect on you.

Your team is therefore a critical extension of yourself. How you manage what is a cohort of ambassadors becomes a critical aspect of delivering overall performance.

*Your goal in managing your leadership team is to create a group which represents fully a **united view of objectives, strategy and values**.*

Context

Teams function most effectively when each team member is seen to be an authority in their own area. In part this determines your approach – you must have the humility to say, and to *believe*, that each of your direct reports should be more expert in their given area than you are. You should understand that your role is not to be the overall expert – a king of all trades – but to enable each of your team members to be a star. This approach is likely to be credible when:

■ you are seen to defer to the specific knowledge of individuals, challenging not their expertise but their reasoning;

■ you *say* in public that your role is not to be an expert.

The use of extensive delegation and the approach to issue-solving assist in this process. A significant role of an effective leader is to assist in problem-solving, but where you are seen as the problem-solver of first resort, then the dependency culture created undermines the specialism of the team member, and with it the effectiveness of the team as a whole. By delegating responsibility in the first instance to your team members, and by indicating that you expect your involvement to be problem-solving of the *last* resort, you enable your team members to gain internal self-esteem and external 'face'. Sometimes this means that you must allow decisions you disagree with – the assumption of responsibility gained by the team member outweighing the downside of the decision.

Challenge

The greatest challenge to a team is managing conflict. Open and constructive disagreement is healthy and should be encouraged. What should be discouraged is stand-offs – significantly different views that become more, not less, entrenched through debate, increasingly personalised, and where the act of opposition becomes more the issue than the real issue itself! In such a circumstance you must cut to the quick, distil the real points of difference and challenge the disputants to resolve the issue based on your distillation of the facts. The ideal outcome is an agreed resolution, though you will not shirk – and your team will know this – from imposing a resolution if needs be. In this, as in all aspects of team management, effective leaders know how to move, and when.

Success

For a team to be effective, it has to be a team in practice, not simply in name. There are a number of techniques you can adopt to ensure that your team operates effectively.

- **Regular meetings** – your team should meet on a regular basis, preferably weekly, on a day and at a time that fits the organisation's cycle. Such a meeting should be issues-based, and strictly limited in time. When you start such a cycle of meetings, the ground rules should be established clearly. A key rule is that no member of the team should be discouraged from expressing a view on any subject or function.

- **Issue meetings** – team meetings should be separated from deeper discussions on key issues (which might also involve other staff), and you have to sense when these should be chaired by yourself, or by a function head, and indeed when you should abstain from attendance altogether. Functional heads must be seen by their own teams as leaders in their own right, and this can be impaired if you dominate proceedings.

- **121s** – group meetings should be supplemented by regular meetings between you and each of your direct reports. Obviously this serves the purpose of monitoring progress regularly on key objectives, but it also allows for a wider-ranging discussion of the business and its performance. Paradoxically, as this *is* a one-to-one, it will contribute to overall team performance because it will help to secure a series of individual relationships on which the team is based.

- **Awaydays** – teams can also be strengthened by the careful use of off-site opportunities for longer periods of undisturbed analysis and reflection. Leaving aside their precise nature and construction, they will deepen team bonds and performance by enabling outside-the-box thinking and by forging stronger personal relationships.

Leaders' measures of success

→ Regular leadership team meetings are scheduled weekly.

→ Regular awayday retreats occur, preferably at least annually.

→ Regular 121s are carried out monthly.

Pitfalls

Above all else treat your team *as* a team. If the team breaks down into a collection of individuals, working in different directions or competing with each other, then the necessary focus on performance delivery will be lost. Team effectiveness will most likely be imperilled if you:

- are seen to treat individuals differently;

- are seen to make decisions in apparently random sub-teams;

- fail to hold regular team meetings and other team-developing events;

- consistently ignore the advice of colleagues and apply a wholly autocratic decision-making style.

Team development is hard. Leaders will almost inevitably experience some element of the *forming–storming–norming–performing* cycle in the development of their leadership team. Avoiding the most obvious pitfalls demands tireless attention to the detail of team management.

Leaders' checklist

- See your team as a group of ambassadors.

- Encourage each team member to believe and understand that in very different ways they champion customer needs.

- Set clear expectations for team behaviour, both in regular meetings and in personal relationships.

- Go out of your way to emphasise your own dependence on the specialist skills of your team.

- Encourage healthy debate, but discourage silo mentalities and partisanship.

- Remember that successful businesses are always greater than the sum of their parts, and that this depends on constructive collaboration.

- Organise periodic social events that bring team members together in a non-formal setting. Even if the talk is still about work, such gatherings help to cement relationships by removing some of the veneer of workplace personae.

121s

A 121 is a regular 'update' meeting between two people, alone and uninterrupted, and is part of the communications and performance management strategy.

Frequency – monthly.
Key participants – direct reports.
Leadership rating ***

Objective

The overall purpose of your communication strategy is to ensure that your organisation's Vision, goals and strategic objectives are communicated to everyone who needs to hear them – and that they are communicated with a frequency and consistency that make it evident that they are serious and authentic. The commitment to deliver such messages to a wide range of staff is a demanding and time-consuming one, but is imperative if strategy and goals are to be credible.

A key element of effective performance is ensuring that all team members' performances are at a level consistent with the core profile of their role and the objectives they have been set to support the team's strategy.

121s are a personal, face-to-face realisation of these communication and performance management objectives. They are the recognition that the effective functioning of a business unit depends on you adopting strategies that bind the team together as a *team*, and also create a foundation for successful one-to-one personal relationships.

*You use 121s to enable **clear and effective communication and performance feedback.***

Context

121s are part of your communications and performance strategies, including:

- regular meetings with your immediate direct reports;
- regular communications/updates with all staff via e-mail;
- participation in regular staff meetings – the frequency of these will depend on the scale and geographical structure of the organisation;
- occasional awaydays for direct reports;
- ongoing feedback – written as well as verbal;
- formal annual appraisals.

The 121 takes its place as a key tool in personalising, regularising and standardising communication and performance management.

Challenge

All the members of a team will be aware that their positions depend on both their individual performance and the effectiveness of their relationship with their leader. Some will seek to bend your ear with their particular views and hope to gain disproportionate influence. Some leaders like it this way and play the team discordantly – setting members up against each other and deriving effectiveness from interpersonal tension. The alternative approach is *collegiate* – you are seen:

- to treat all members of the team equally;
- to accord to each individual equivalent respect for the legitimacy of their opinions;
- to ensure that decision-making processes apply consistently to all team members;
- to encourage healthy and open debate where differences of opinion are respected and debated rigorously, not rancorously.

By utilising 121s on a regular basis, you will provide a structure which meets the need for regular communication and consistent feedback with all your team members on a common basis.

Success

There are four main components of the effective 121.

- **A general discussion of 'how things are going'** – this may sound woolly but the goal is to provide the opportunity to take the temperature of the organisation and particular personal relationships and, most importantly, to allow an individual to raise broad concerns and issues.

- **A review of personal objectives** – objectives should be set for the year as a whole, and it is unlikely they should each be specifically reviewed on a monthly basis. Nonetheless, the 121 does provide an opportunity for selective review – not least because it is in your own interests that you and your staff meet their goals, and that performance issues are dealt with promptly.

- **A discussion of current specific business issues** – these will vary at different points in time. The key here is that you are engaging in the right ones – i.e. those where discussion adds value. The benefits are:

  - your colleagues see you engaging in their area of competence;

  - you can take the opportunity to learn from others' specific skills and knowledge;

  - you can take the opportunity to reinforce key strategies;

  - you reinforce your approach to problem-solving and decision-making.

- **Discussions about the next level of staff** – i.e. your direct reports' direct reports. This will lead in many directions but there will be two main benefits:

- providing you with a regular insight into the performance of the group, which should be central to your thinking about succession planning;

- counselling direct reports on performance issues *they* are facing.

It is essential that 121s are followed-up by written action points. Such actions should be followed up no later than the next monthly 121.

Leaders' measures of success

→ The number of 121s held per year per direct report.

→ Written notes are completed after each meeting, and reviewed the next.

→ An independent assessment is carried out by your HR executive into whether known performance issues have been tackled or not.

Pitfalls

If 121s are vital to performance management and communication, then not doing them at all, or doing them inconsistently, will undermine your commitment to excellence on a range of issues. There are three main risks with 121s.

- **You regularly cancel 121s or don't do them at all** – to avoid this, you must train yourself to understand that they are as significant as (say) financial monthly reports, whose timely completion by the accounts team is not normally negotiable.

- **The 121s lack structure and/or an agenda** – this will indicate that they mean little. You should always ensure that the team member is given a list of discussion items.

- **The leader glosses over personal performance issues** – raising personal issues can be uncomfortable, and avoidance raises the likelihood of sub-optimal performance. So if confrontation is an issue you should consider providing feedback with the HR executive involved.

Leaders' checklist

- Remember that 121s send an important signal about your commitment to communication and feedback, so organise them on at least a monthly basis, and on a rolling basis looking forward at least six months.

- Allow at least an hour per session – much less time inhibits detailed discussion.

- Make sure that 121s are also scheduled for any staff who might be based overseas – for these (who may feel remote) your 121s assume an even greater importance.

- Prepare for all 121s by making a list of points to discuss to ensure that the 121 has a structure, including a review of action items from the previous meeting.

- If the meeting is likely to include performance feedback, you might want to discuss the issues with your relevant HR executive – personal feedback can be difficult, and rehearsing the issue with an experienced professional allows you to ensure that your concerns are well-grounded, and also to test out the sensitivity and effectiveness of your approach.

- Encourage your direct report to give feedback about you and your role – reciprocal feedback will create an atmosphere of trust, which will in turn facilitate a more open discussion of issues.

- Ensure where possible that the 121 takes place in a private environment and that you won't be disturbed.

Your team is more skilled than you

Your key area of expertise is leadership – in most everything else you should aim to have a team of individuals more highly skilled than yourself.

Frequency – every personal interaction!
Key participants – direct reports.
Leadership rating: Leadership6

Objective

Whatever team you are responsible for – at whatever level, in whatever business, in whatever function – it is absolutely vital that you do not confuse *leadership skills* with *functional skills*. Leadership is an art that demands intensive understanding, development and practice across a wide range of essentially interpersonal activities. To the extent that I am attempting to explain these, leadership is its own discipline – what it is *not* is a replacement for the very considerable and detailed functional skills normally required in any specific part of a business.

I have indicated elsewhere how significant a priority it is for you to select the right individuals for your team. Core to this selection process is identifying individuals who are more expert than you in their given area; and core to maintaining your team's effectiveness is privately and publicly ensuring that these superior skills are recognised and heralded.

*Your objective is to be **first among equals** as leader, **last among equals** as functional specialist.*

Context

Sometimes (perhaps very often) this approach to competence is painful – making decisions oneself, or delegating them to nominated individuals, is much simpler than balancing the knowledge of varying groups. But if you can get this approach right, your team members will feel they are contributing when they should. And if you can make your focus the process of enabling this then they will realise that their inclusion is based first and foremost on their skills and experience and not seniority, title or status. This, then, becomes a source of a satisfying feeling of personal value.

With this approach in place, you will realise that leadership is not about knowing more than your team. To the contrary, it is about the humility of recognising that you know less. It is not about leading through the example of having the answers to everything, but through delivering superior performance by orchestrating above-average collective insight. It means that leadership is about delivering an extraordinarily challenging, and sometimes near-impossible, balance – that while you must put yourself forward charismatically to drive the Vision and purpose, you should, if anything, put yourself in the intellectual background.

Challenge

Many business issues are multi-faceted and complex, even on a day-to-day basis, and demand integrated and sophisticated answers. Very frequently we find that superior performance is delivered by the organisations that have thought these issues through the most carefully. But what we also know is that many of these increasingly sophisticated responses are being made with increasing speed. As business leaders we then face the challenge of delivering the ever more complex ever more rapidly.

There are two alternative leadership styles to this challenge, which I believe are increasingly unlikely to be effective.

- **Directive leader** – the one we have probably all met, the one who not only likes to use leadership as a platform for the extensive articulation of opinions, but who likes to direct what happens. This is the individual who comes to believe that leadership confers experience across all disciplines and whose raison d'être is action – to be seen in the driving seat, to be seen making decisions. Such a leadership, based on ego and willpower, while it can be extremely effective at the individual decision level, will become increasingly distanced from the detailed knowledge required to confront a multiplicity of issues.

- **Empowering leader** – who believes in empowerment as a liberating mantra but who, in correctly identifying the energising effect of bestowing responsibility on the individual, may overlook the more powerful synergies that arise from combining different individuals' skills collaboratively (and which requires some constraints of empowerment).

What is required instead, to confront complex challenges, is an approach that *pools* knowledge and experience in a cross-functional and non-hierarchical manner.

Success

Successful sharing of knowledge does not mean that organisations become some form of brains trust, paralysed into inaction through the continual intensity of analysis. Nor does it mean that decision-making should be done by standing committee. It means that in confronting issues your team should expect to work with the following principles.

- **Customer-led focus** – you communicate, as a first principle, that issues should never be seen in a departmental context but always with a business-wide customer-led focus.
- **Flexibility** – you ensure that while the whole team is aware of the current major challenges, they are also aware that problem-solving will always be undertaken by drawing on the required skills case by case.
- **Ad hoc teams** – you create ad hoc teams time and time again, relentlessly so, to deal with ongoing challenges.

- **Brief** – you set these teams a clear brief with a clear timetable to deliver recommended solutions.
- **Your role** – you chart your role as an organiser and final evaluator, not a prime mover of the analysis itself.
- **Removing obstacles** – you ensure that any resource or attitude constraints are removed.

This approach will be further augmented by the way you enable your team members to work together. When they see that their participation in problem-solving is based on their ability to contribute, so they will develop a greater respect for each other's competence, and also realise the extent to which they can learn from each other – that, in effect, their personal value is interdependent.

Leaders' measures of success

The extent to which your team members present solutions rather than problems.

The speed with which issues are brought to resolution.

The number of unresolved issues at any one time.

Pitfalls

There is a balance to be struck between sharing ideas and decision-making – too much of the former can impede the latter! While team members will want (and deserve) respect for their own skills, they will also want to see effective decision-making. They are unlikely to be motivated by a leadership style so humble and deferential that issue resolution is avoided. So you must avoid:

- overly consensual decision-making where too much allowance (and time) is made for conflicting views;
- a culture in which respect for opinion means that everyone offers an opinion on everything;

■ any feeling that because your team members are functional specialists they are not expected to display leadership characteristics.

This is a tough balance. As an effective leader you will learn when to encourage opinion or when to impose a decision, when to encourage or when to end debate, when to stand back and when to take the lead on an issue.

Leaders' checklist

■ However much you articulate your sense of leadership in driving your business forward, never articulate the idea that you have all the answers – articulate instead that you are there to provide a framework (a working culture) for others to find solutions.

■ Try to exclude yourself, where you can, from the immediate processes that are being used to tackle issues (unless they are of such strategic significance that your absence would be construed as negligence) – be seen to stand back and let the experts take the lead.

■ Use 121s with your direct reports to learn about their areas of functional specialism – let them know that you want to learn and that you see them as having a crucial role in this respect.

■ Have a bias towards using ad hoc rather than standing teams to confront issues so that you always apply the skills needed for the challenge.

■ Recognise success in your team publicly and regularly – and never take the credit for others' ideas.

Team members in other countries

Some leaders have direct reports in overseas countries. This presents challenges of distance and (potentially) time difference which require special attention and foresight.

Frequency – sporadic.
Key participants – probably a limited number of direct reports.
Leadership rating **

Objective

Anyone who has ever been based in a country away from head office – especially one with a significant time-zone change – will probably already know that it is a significant and formative experience. There may have been a sense of liberation from HQ bureaucracy, and a greater feeling of entrepreneurship from being close to developing markets. There may also have been an opportunity to gain a broader commercial experience by managing functions (e.g. HR, facilities, finance) that in HQ were central services.

The experience can also have significantly negative aspects:

- for a 'local' team member – the challenges of different business cultures, knowledge and possibly language, and a lack of familiarity with the organisation's home-country culture;

- for the expat team member – the challenge of different 'resident country' culture and business practices, isolation from the organisation's home-country centre of gravity, and probably remoteness from the family.

*As a leader of overseas-based staff you have a major responsibility to ensure that you pursue your goals on a common basis, while respecting the **specific challenges arising in different countries**.*

Context

As a leader of any business activity with an international scope, you must be acutely aware of your organisation's strategic positioning (export, international, global or glocal – see p. 62). On a day-to-day basis this will inform who is employed as key team members in other countries, where they come from and with what experience, and what performance expectations are set for them.

Some factors which influence choice of key team members include:

- whether the international operation is 'representative' or 'trading' – each has different commercial requirements;
- what languages are required for business transactions;
- the level of interaction with governmental and regulatory organisations – this affects the requirement for skills in negotiation and diplomacy;
- the balance between general-market and industry-specific knowledge;
- the scale of the business operation and associated levels of support – this affects the extent to which a key team member needs to be 'self-starting';
- how frequently you expect to be able to meet the team member face-to-face – this may drive the required level of independence;
- whether previous international organisation experience is required.

Immediately you will see that the process of employing staff outside your home base is significantly complex.

Challenge

The starting point is for you to *acknowledge* that there *are* differences if you have team members in other countries. This is a complex set of differences because the overseas team member may belong to one of four categories:

- from the organisation's home country and employed overseas as an expat;
- from the organisation's home country and employed on a local basis;
- from the country where they are based;
- from neither the organisation's home country nor where they are based.

This variety is becoming increasingly common as more business people are educated internationally, and work and travel internationally. Each of the four categories above brings with it its own set of unique challenges.

- **Culture** – the issues, and stresses, associated with working in a foreign culture, especially for a manager doing this for the first time.
- **Family** – the associated stresses related to moving families – notably education, health and childcare.
- **Spouses and partners** – the particular issues relating to spouses who themselves may have to give up their jobs to move, sometimes to new locations where work permits are difficult to obtain.
- **Finance** – the major financial implications for expats arising from working abroad. These are often very positive but can be undermined by inadequate advice and planning for tax, pensions and social security.
- **Global strategy** – the challenges that can arise in attempting to implement global strategies and values in environments where business is conducted differently, and the expectations of senior managers vary.
- **Regional strategy** – the challenge for senior managers in *regional* international roles, where they may face as many differences in cultures within their regions as there are between their regions and the culture in the home country.

If you are responsible for sending or 'posting' a colleague to another country, it is vital that your commitment to supporting them starts with the relocation process. This means ensuring that:

- the remuneration package suitably reflects the environment to which the direct report is being moved;
- they have an adequate chance to assess the fairness of what is being proposed – say in terms of cost of living;
- they recognise that tax, pensions and social security planning assistance is probably necessary;
- you set time frames and work expectations that reflect the demands of moving a family (if this is the case).

Success

For your team members based in other countries, it is vitally important that they feel in the loop. In many cases, being involved in running businesses away from head office will offer them a blend of:

- the greater challenges associated with a wider span of control;
- the enhanced freedom of doing things in the way they want.

But cutting across this will be their feeling of not wanting to be isolated. Your response must be to feel that you are overcommunicating, remembering the maxim that 'you can never overcommunicate'. You will have to compensate for the personal distance created by physical distance with some artificiality and excess in the 'inclusive' strategies you implement. These will include:

- **121s** – organising a weekly telephone one-to-one, less to deal with ongoing objectives or issues, more to provide a relatively fixed point in the calendar to touch base and identify any general concerns.
- **Meetings** – including overseas direct reports in all relevant meetings, by telephone, videoconference or WebEx, is a matter of course not exception.

■ **HQ visits** – invite direct reports to periodic meetings in the home country to ensure that personal relationships with colleagues are maintained.

■ **In-country visits** – plan regular visits to your direct reports' overseas locations to demonstrate to them and *their* own staff that your view of international business is not based exclusively on views from head office and/or by summoning staff there.

Some of this may sound obvious or even trivial, but its importance cannot be overestimated – the goal here is to ensure that staff based overseas feel and believe that they are being accommodated, listened to and included. This approach will be seen as insubstantial and superficial if it is transitory. If, however, you make it a permanent part of your leadership modus operandi, it will be credible and you will be seen to be truly international.

Leaders' measures of success

→ Overseas team members are included in all staff meetings (e.g. by phone) or communicated to separately.

→ Overseas team members' 121s are scheduled and implemented.

→ Overseas team members' countries are visited, and they are met face-to-face at least once a year.

Pitfalls

Staff working in different time zones may often be on the receiving end of what appears to be thoughtless actions from managers back home. For example:

■ phone calls at home, at apparently random times;

■ requests to participate in teleconferences at impossibly early or late times of the day;

■ teleconferences, meetings or visits scheduled with no regard for differences in public holidays or customs;

- e-mail and other correspondence in terms not suited to local cultures;
- business processes not tailored to individual market requirements;
- employment arrangements following company 'standards' rather than customised to suit market requirements;
- sales and marketing planning processes too head office 'centre' driven rather than based on local market insights.

These are just some of many common examples that could be listed – they are all avoidable.

The moral for leaders with team members in other countries is to be aware that effective sensitivity to cultural difference depends on attention to detail.

Leaders' checklist

- Always bear in mind that no matter how the world looks from your office, the 'centre' is only where you choose it to be and the world looks very different from other locations.

- Ensure that all overseas managers reporting to you have appropriate employment terms – dissatisfaction about terms is extremely corrosive and is magnified when staff are at a distance.

- Be aware that when it comes to managing overseas locations, actions really do speak louder than words. You have to be seen to be engaged, you have to be visible, you have to be seen to be learning from different places and cultures.

- Even as you seek to create an international business with common strategies and values, you have to talk the *language of difference* – respecting difference for the value it creates.

- Speak with your direct reports regularly – paradoxically, perhaps even more regularly than with the staff based in your location.

four

Leading your organisation

As a leader you may have a broader team than your direct reports – your span of responsibility may extend into their own teams and their own direct reports. Whether this overall team can be counted in the tens or the hundreds, you must be aware that you are addressing – in your goals, strategies, actions and words – a much wider audience than just your direct reports. For this much larger and disparate audience you must have practical activity and communication techniques that are *deliberately* designed to:

- **reinforce** goals, strategies and targets;

- **inculcate** in the organisation your view of the business world and the way you do business;

- **change** your organisation's culture in ways you feel appropriate;

- **challenge** legacy assumptions that may impede future development and performance;

- **inform** staff about business performance;
- **solicit** explicit feedback on the business, its performance and culture.

If this makes leadership sound like a *performance*, it is – as I say elsewhere, this is not about acting or phoniness, but about putting yourself 'out there' to be seen and heard. This requires commitment, effort, determination, resilience and patience. Winning or changing hearts and minds does not come easily – your successes will have to be earned.

In an increasingly commoditised and volatile business environment, there has never been a greater need for leaders who are able to marshal excellent performance, where leadership is not an end in itself but focuses on the energising and optimisation of an organisation's major differentiation – their human capital. In this sense, then, the leader sits not at the *top* of a classic pyramidal hierarchy, but *beneath* a vast array of superior talent.

Your challenge is to be effective through people – to deliver transformational performance by unlocking individuals' potential. Your leadership is paradoxically at once *centre-stage* because you orchestrate performance excellence; but also *back-stage*, because your leadership creates platforms for others.

So as a leader you are an advocate for your cause, paradoxically creating more opportunity for others by relentlessly evangelising your own ideas.

Credibility from repetition

Effective leaders must be seen and heard – for their leadership messages to be believed, they must be repeated remorselessly.

Frequency – constant.
Key participants – all staff and partners.
Leadership rating: Leadership6

Objective

Leaders are agents of action – they want to achieve, and to be seen to achieve. You know that you will need the support of all your staff, often in confronting difficult circumstances and decisions. You want your staff to understand where their business is heading, why and how. You must recognise that this direction and purpose has to be communicated clearly amid the many other messages that staff hear on a day-to-day basis. You must also be realistic that all colleagues bring with them assumptions, or even prejudices, many deeply ingrained.

So as an effective leader you must learn very rapidly that a key instrument in communicating your ambitions, for them to be heard by the crowd and for them to win hearts and minds, is *repetition*. Constant acts of reinforcement serve two purposes:

- they grab *mindshare* and attention – your messages are heard;
- they win *credibility* – you are heard so often that you are taken seriously.

*As leader you must **exceed every expectation** you have about communicating your key messages – you will not begin to communicate enough until you feel you are doing too much.*

Context

The effective leader is a figurehead. As I have already remarked, your every move is closely scrutinised. As you set the tone for your organisation – from key values to the way you deal with people, be they staff or partners – your words are an exceptionally strong currency. While the most effective leader cannot be anything but natural, you must learn naturally to select words carefully and thoughtfully. What is important is less *how much* is said, than *what* is said – and the 'what' must be strategic in its own right:

- it supports the Vision and strategy;
- it is clear and interpretable;
- it is consistent and unambiguous;
- it is actionable.

All these features must bear the hallmark of repetition. In other words, you communicate the same message repetitively to achieve the same effect. In this way, your staff have a clear business compass on which they can depend and in which they can invest trust.

Challenge

It is the nature of business structures (of all sizes) that leadership changes. You cannot assume that you have the prospect of longevity in your role to allow you to craft and reinforce your messages over long periods of time. You should also be aware that your teams may become cynical about leadership 'vision', since they may have seen leaders – and messages – come and go with increasingly undermining regularity. Change and scepticism thus represent major challenges – *do you have the time to sustain a convincing messaging which overcomes natural barriers of suspicion?*

You will soon realise that in establishing and maintaining credibility, you face a unique intersection of issues:

- **legacy** – the position left by your predecessor, and especially its impact on your team's willingness to embrace the Vision;
- **time** – the need to make rapid impacts in a potentially volatile environment;
- **style** – your ability to communicate effectively and quickly;
- **Vision** – your readiness to share your intelligible but stretching view of the future;
- **stamina** – your ability to communicate relentlessly but without loss of enthusiasm;
- **change** – how you face change but communicate consistently.

The pull of character and circumstance may drive you to be cautious about commitments. The best leaders, however, face down caution with bravery, set out their stall and stick with it.

Success

'Sticking with it' is the key. You must have immense self-belief in what you are doing, not only in espousing a clear Vision, strategy and set of goals but in *saying so*. Not only in being a leader, but acting as one.

This means that you take each and every opportunity to repeat and reinforce your key messages.

- **Strategic and annual plans** include a restatement of the core Vision, strategy and goals.
- **Intranet and internet** websites broadcast key messages to a wide partner and public audience.
- **Every management, team or staff meeting** is seen as a forum for messages to be repeated.
- **Memos or announcements** sent to staff link core goals to advertised developments or changes.
- **121s** link personal development objectives to broader goals.

■ **External events** (conference speeches, stands) and **media events** (interviews, articles) enable public reinforcement of corporate goals and messages.

In truth, you must live the life of the Vision, strategy and goals you set so strongly that you come to embody them. This is an intensely personalised leadership that uses the power of your individuality – your charisma, drive and persuasion – to prose-lytise a view of the future. To some extent this is driven by you alone, it represents risk – but to the very same extent it is the power of personality that truly leads by example.

Leaders' measures of success

➤ Vision, strategy and goals are referred to in all strategy plans, staff meetings, team meetings and 121s.

➤ You refer to Vision, strategy and goals at least once a day.

➤ You listen to hear Vision, strategy and goals being repeated by your team unprompted – the more they do this, the more it has all sunk in!

Pitfalls

There is little more dangerous to a leader than confused commu-nication – if business direction is underpinned by a clear Vision and strategy, then it can just as easily lose value if it is not under-stood by everyone. There are three main risks:

■ **weak messages** – a lack of reinforcement will render messages unimportant and undifferentiated, and the audience will be unable to identify what is significant and special;

■ **too many messages** – irrespective of how frequently they are reinforced, too many messages will confuse an audience because focus and prioritisation will be ambiguous;

■ **changing messages** – if key messages change, the audience will 'learn' to ignore future messages because they will lack belief in the substance of messaging.

These pitfalls reinforce how critical it is for you as leader to be certain about the key messages you want to convey – to communicate with a determination and relentlessness, and always to feel that you are overcommunicating.

Leaders' checklist

■ Always remember that you are a personal representation of the Vision, strategy and goals you have created or support – your demeanour counts!

■ Remember too that you are also a personification of values – the way you act and the way you speak will say as much about your values as any published memo on values ever can.

■ Distil your Vision, strategy and goals into key messages to be reinforced throughout your business life.

■ Understand that you have to take each and every opportunity to communicate your key messages, and know that you will feel you are doing this too much – if you don't feel this, you are definitely communicating too little!

■ Know that your time may be limited – so communicate regularly and clearly from day one in the job, even if at the start you are communicating values and laying the groundwork for more definitive statements later.

Resistance to change

'We have always done things this way' is an example of a statement made in resistance to change – you must be acutely sensitive to such signals and demonstrate that you don't accept them.

Frequency – constant reinforcement.
Key participants – everyone you meet.
Leadership rating ****

Objective

Nothing should irritate you more than statements such as:

- 'this is the way we do things here';
- 'this has always worked for other clients';
- 'we have always done things this way'.

Hearing any one of them should be like a red rag to a bull, and – fairly or unfairly – always lead you to believe that whoever is making the statements is defending a status quo that is ripe for change.

Leadership is always and inevitably about change – this is, of course, your leadership perspective. But it is also about others *accepting* the inevitability of change.

*As you engage in your organisation, you must be acutely aware of **resistance to change**, however it is expressed.*

Context

If your role is about forcing change, and your team's role is to accept the inevitability of change, then this will in turn provoke some clashes between openness and defensiveness. When you hear the words 'we have always done things this way' or (in response to a suggested change) 'we don't do things like that here', what you are actually witnessing is:

- resistance, because change is just hard;
- defensiveness because of individuals' concerns that their credibility will be undermined;
- complacency because of an essential lack of motivation;
- fear about changes to roles, and potential loss of employment.

These responses will often be deeply rooted, especially where they betray vulnerability. Responding will demand from you a conviction and steadfastness that will be frequently challenged and undermined, and you will need to maintain focus on long-term goals rather than short-term ups-and-downs.

Challenge

You should always be prepared for the status quo to take hold – even one you have been instrumental in creating. So you must be attuned to hearing defensiveness when you are demanding change – and you should always insist on change in a business environment where success will depend on continuous improvement.

When you hear statements that implicitly or explicitly say 'we don't understand why you want to do things differently', you must expose how such statements are riddled with blindness to the need for change. You must stress, and *be heard* to say, that:

- the onus is always on a leader to demand change, and on their staff to respond openly;
- to concentrate on how previous things have worked successfully is never a wholly adequate answer to moving forward;
- to cite established processes and procedures suggests that change should conform to them, rather than the processes being adapted to the needs of change.

No leader ever wants to convey the impression they are impervious to others' views, nor that there are no legitimate challenges to their opinions. But when you are fixed on your purpose, you must be single-minded in your determination to meet resistance with both conviction and an irrepressible belief in success.

Success

So how do leaders challenge resistance to change successfully and also ensure that they themselves never become the status quo that is itself the problem?

First you challenge your team. You must believe and be heard to say that that no matter how successful the team has been, how much market share it has achieved and how thoroughly it feels it understands its market, its dynamics and structures, it must continuously reassess its competitive positioning. The team must be aware of:

- **complacency** – success may breed a dangerous complacency;
- **the status quo** – reliance on this reveals a failure to understand that all business involves a continuous journey;
- **continuous change** – change is not something you do every so often, it is a corporate way of life.

And the team must know that these factors apply to it no less than to its competitors.

Next you challenge yourself. Building a business or a team is an arduous and stressful process, albeit an exhilarating one. Along the way you take risks, face major hurdles and invest a great deal in building your team. It will be an emotional rollercoaster, frequently challenging your stamina, your self-belief and your will-power. Establishing a status quo as a safe haven is undeniably attractive, but recognising this very attractiveness is the key to avoiding being one of those 'we always do it this way' businesses. As an effective leader, you spurn safety for danger, status quo for change. However demanding this may be, it means:

- **getting out** – you never cease meeting players in their world to spot emerging trends;
- **standing back** – you regularly do this to assess the appropriateness of your organisation's strategy to market needs;
- **assessing management** – you constantly assess the effectiveness of your management structure;
- **challenging** – you relentlessly challenge the 'customer journey' and demand to see customer complaints so that you know from the coalface what may not be working;
- **listening** – you listen to what your colleagues really *say* for evidence of 'we always do it this way' attitudes;
- **investing** – you invest in time with customers and *listen* to what they say about your organisation's performance, and ensure that improvement processes are driven by customer perspectives;
- **refreshing** – you face the reality, hard as it may be, that your close-knit team will itself need refreshing with new approaches and attitudes.

Above all, you have to display humble self-awareness – an openness to change that accepts that constant change is not a reflection of failure, but is your responsibility.

Leaders' measures of success

→ How often do you have to challenge change-resistant statements?

→ How often are you having to emphasise change programmes in response to defensiveness?

→ How high are you scoring on customer satisfaction surveys?

Pitfalls

You must guard against being so driven towards improvement that change itself becomes problematic. So beware of the following.

- **The leader excessively criticises the past** – if it is the 'past' that is described as the problem, rather than specific features of it, then you may imply that all previous ideas and experience have low value, and you may unintentionally suppress or sacrifice significant knowledge and insights.

- **The leader excessively criticises staff associated with the past** – signals that people associated with the past may, by definition, be a problem will devalue their legitimate experience and may undermine their commitment to support change; precisely the reverse outcome to the desired one.

- **Reactions to the status quo are overhasty** – knee-jerk reactions to perceived inadequacies may feel good, but you always need to learn why things are as they are; a failure to grasp hidden complexities actually undermines the change process.

- **Overinsistence on change at the expense of praise** – commentary on an organisation's culture and performance should be balanced. If you appear biased towards blaming error, then respect for you as a leader will be undermined; staff will always accept challenge and some criticism when it is evenly balanced with deserved praise.

Leaders' checklist

- From your first day as leader, emphasise the importance of change and be humble enough to acknowledge when you yourself are making changes.

- Talk about change positively – embed it in the organisation's culture as a norm, not an event.

- Be brave in regularly standing back from a business in which you may have invested emotionally – ask yourself what would be your perspective if you were new.

- Always solicit feedback from customers and find ways of

demonstrating that their feedback has been noted and actioned.

- If you ever hear your staff talking about 'we always do it this way', make it clear that such approaches are wholly unacceptable.

Process: making the right things happen at the right time

Successful businesses are managed every step of the way. The effective leader knows that process is the key to making the right things happen at the right time.

Frequency – embedded in operations continuously.
Key participants – all staff.
Leadership rating **

Objective

'Process' describes a planned sequence of events for a given circumstance. The mere suggestion of it may turn many leaders off because it implies an attention to planned detail and structure that may seem the very opposite of the flair and excitement of leadership. Some may believe that detailed process belongs to the realms of technology-intensive engineering or manufacturing.

But consider five, apparently quite unconnected, challenges requiring specific, timetabled and planned outcomes:

- making staff redundant in a manner consistent with employment legislation;
- the launch of a major new product on time and to budget;
- the delivery of quarter-by-quarter sales on target;
- answering customer complaints about poor service and providing appropriate apologies or recompense;
- transfer of staff from one office location to another on time and on budget.

All these examples involve different groups of employees (respectively HR, product development, sales, customer service and facilities) and yet they must all meet clear, and in many cases cost-sensitive, deadlines. They will best meet these successfully if they have a clear idea of what is required and when, and who is doing it.

Your objective across all your staff is to ensure they understand that goals are best met – whether for one-off projects or ongoing activities – when tasks are clearly mapped within **process structures***.*

Context

All businesses have a simple goal – delivering the highest revenue at the lowest cost. This is achieved through some core steps:

- identification of market opportunities;
- creation and delivery of products and services;
- appropriate after-sales service and support.

Managing what becomes a development–sales–support 'cycle' demands a preoccupation with the allocation of resources – put simply, where and when to invest most wisely, and how to deliver an optimum level of sales and margin. This budgetary preoccupation is, however, sometimes too often focused on what is spent rather than how it is spent – attempts to reduce costs, for example, often focus on supplier cost reduction programmes or staff retrenchment rather than on why cost is being incurred.

An organisation or business unit should understand which actions it is taking that incur cost. It should see these in the eyes of its customers (internal and external) and ask if they are receiving the service they require. It should also ask itself what cost is being incurred through remedying past failures, poor decisions or faulty planning.

Confronting the extent to which costs are being incurred as a price of failure (sometimes called 'the cost of quality') should be your priority. These include:

- sales lost through inadequate products or poor sales delivery;
- excessive costs incurred through confusion or duplication of processes;

■ costs incurred in remedying after-sales faults and complaints.

You should never accept today's costs as the legitimate costs for your business or function. You should challenge your team to appraise their processes – the organisation of their actions – so that they deliver 'right first time' across all teams.

Challenge

There are two types of negative reactions to the concept of process. The first is emotional – 'process' sounds dull. Rigorous attention to detail can seem unexciting and bureaucratic. Worse, it may suggest a 'playing by the book' mentality that discourages risk and entrepreneurship.

Not attending to appropriate process is an easy way out, and a quick one. Not anticipating consequences reveals a 'mañana' attitude. Above all else, responding to the challenges and dramas that arise from a lack of process can actually be exciting. For certain kinds of staff, riding to the rescue in a tough situation is more motivating than engaging in detailed planning to avoid the problem in the first place.

The second type of challenge to process is an organisational–cultural one, and it affects organisations in three distinct phases.

■ **Start-up** – for a new business, process may seem a luxury amidst the hurly-burly of getting going and keeping afloat.

■ **Growth enterprise** – for a business growing quickly, it may find it difficult to keep its processes aligned to the demands of its customers, and not know how to keep going and take stock at the same time.

■ **Mature business** – for an established business, the paradox may be that it does have established processes but they are the wrong ones. The appearance of an established process may actually have become a barrier to successful delivery.

Your role as leader is to understand and articulate the power of process irrespective of the phase your organisation or team is in and to demonstrate instead its overriding value. Your special challenge is to show how process does not undermine being smart, nimble or entrepreneurial – rather that process *is* smart, nimble and entrepreneurial.

Success

If the primacy of process is successfully understood, a given team will:

- **question** whether process is relevant to a particular activity or not;
- **embed** process in any activity rather than see it as a separate, optional add-on;
- **define and record** a process for a given activity, with specified accountabilities;
- **automate process steps** where this is achievable and acceptable to stakeholders;
- **extend** the process to include external suppliers and customers;
- **review** the process with stakeholders before implementing it, if it is new;
- **continuously re-engineer** the given process based on feedback;
- **create Key Performance Indicators (KPIs)** to measure the process;
- **train** staff where appropriate in using the given process;
- **calculate** the costs associated with each step in the process.

To reinforce the importance of process, you must say that it is important to all staff, and must constantly reinforce this message through actions and review. Your key messages will be:

- **to use and advocate the term 'process' publicly** – do not shy away from talking about what might be seen as a mundane, boring or technical term;

- **to demand attention to process from your team** – talk about process in your team meetings in the context of overall performance;
- **to require process reviews of all key operational processes** – be seen to engage in the detail of process and do so on a regular basis;
- **to monitor process failures** – know, through formal reporting mechanisms, where process failures are apparent and how they are being addressed;
- **to be unforgiving of failure** – demand a culture of continuous improvement, and show that underachievement is never acceptable;
- **to measure the costs of failure** – failures should not be seen simply as mistakes that can be rectified and re-engineered away; ensure they are seen as having a *cost* that should be measured.

Successful attention to process requires an enormous investment of time. You must also ensure that your team has members who can understand, articulate and lead process – who understand that it is the life-blood of their capacity to succeed.

Leaders' measures of success

→ All teams have process documentation for an agreed set of activities.

→ All teams have ongoing feedback mechanisms for continuous process improvement.

→ Relevant processes are externally certified (e.g. BSI, ISO).

Pitfalls

The importance of process can be undermined in two quite opposite respects.

- **Process and complacency** – the temptation is great for leaders to assume that once processes are in place they can sit back and watch them operate. But process is never finished, it has no end-point. In as much as it demands a relentless attention to detail, it demands a relentless attention to review and renewal. You must expect to focus as much on process change as process implementation to maintain the momentum of continuous improvement. The alternative is that the very process the business heralds becomes its Achilles' heel.

- **Process and atrophy** – without careful explanation, the importance of process may be seen as the primacy of risk-averse planning. In the desire to do things the right way, the business loses its focus on doing the right things. More specifically it might sacrifice its entrepreneurial or creative flair. You must ensure that no one believes that process is a replacement for ideas, but very often a support for their effective realisation.

Much of leadership is actually about the imbalance of relentlessly making the same points time and time again. The approach to process needs to be nuanced – achieving the right attention to focus while remaining creative.

Leaders' checklist

- Talk about process regularly – do not shirk referring to a potentially dull subject.

- Make process commercial – link it to sales and profits so it is never seen as an end in itself.

- Talk about process to your team collectively and to each of your direct reports – don't allow 'process' to be seen as 'belonging' to one particular function or discipline.

- Participate directly in process reviews and seek to know about process failures.

■ Test out processes yourself where it is possible – see them from the customer's perspective.

■ Celebrate process champions – they can all too often be unsung heroes.

Staff meetings

Staff meetings play a huge and often undervalued role in your ability to connect with staff and reinforce key messages.

Frequency – monthly for an immediate team.
Key participants – all the staff you are responsible for.
Leadership rating **

Objective

Personal, one-on-one interaction is a vital part of how you manage your staff – the ability to connect, listen and be seen to learn at an individual level characterises the leader who recognises the value of every team member as unique and distinctive. Equally, you need to manage your team *as a team*, and this represents the very different dynamic of speaking to potentially large groups of people, often in public or semi-public settings. This demands different skills, different preparation and a careful attention to detail. If you are addressing a group, you need to speak about the goals and values that will bring a disparate group of individuals together. This is where leadership really comes into its own, because the leader becomes the public persona – even the icon – for the organisation. Where one-on-one interaction demands the personal touch, so public presentation demands the power and drama of advocacy.

*Effective leaders use staff meetings to **dramatise** and **evangelise** their goals and values.*

Context

You will have to manage a hierarchy of types of personal communication depending on the scale of your responsibility.

- **Informal one-on-one meetings** – generally ad hoc discussions, but always an opportunity to connect personally and to reinforce business approaches and values.
- **Formal 121s** – usually monthly and primarily an opportunity to review ongoing issues, goals and personal performance.
- **Ad hoc group meetings** – to discuss specific, time-defined issues, primary focus analysis and decision-making.
- **Team meetings** – mainly relevant where you lead a single function and bring together your key team members for operational and issue reviews.
- **Management meetings** – weekly, biweekly or monthly reviews (with set agendas) to monitor team performance.
- **Thematic reviews** – periodic reviews, to an agenda and timetable set by you, where you choose periodic assessments of key operational functions.
- **Annual budgeting and planning** – an opportunity to review strategies and cast plans for the next few years.

At the top of this hierarchy sits the *staff meeting* where you address a group larger than your direct reports or immediate team. This is the biggest single opportunity to set the tone for your organisation.

Challenge

Make no mistake – staff meetings can be scary, they can be risky and they can be deflating.

- **Why scary?** Speaking to any large group can be intimidating, and only the most reckless individual fails to recognise the associated stress for what it is. Some leaders are naturally less assured on their feet, and find it off-putting to dramatise – to overemphasise the points they need to make. Some will feel self-conscious and may regard the formality of a public gathering more likely to create distance between them and their staff rather than create bonds.

- **Why risky?** Putting any group of people together is by definition unpredictable, and in any culture of openness it may lead to uncomfortable or unanticipated issues being raised. The risk here is that your agenda may be diverted, though the gains in openness usually outweigh the downsides of frankness.

- **Why deflating?** The opposite to unforeseen discussions can occur – the meetings where there is no response at all. You may feel that your words have fallen on deaf ears. This can be deflating because you may feel that this reflects on either your message or your delivery – though you should remember that your staff may feel as inhibited as you in public gatherings.

These challenges require guts, careful planning and resilience. Above all you must believe in their value, and in the end this belief will see you through.

Success

The most effective staff meetings combine careful planning and attention to detail with a personal touch.

- **Timetabling** – where possible, unless the meeting is for a special announcement, advertise the meeting at least 48 hours in advance to allow staff to (re)schedule their diaries.

- **Advance planning** – if the meetings involve a series, advertise the dates on a rolling six-month basis.

- **Remote attendees** – if staff are dialling-in by teleconference, ensure both that the phone numbers are well advertised (e.g. via Outlook) and that the speaker system is adequate. Up-to-date systems allow meetings to be recorded and uploaded to the internet for absentees.

- **International attendees** – if staff are dialling-in from overseas, be conscious of time differences.

- **Location choice** – obviously this is primarily driven by the size of the meeting. Generally, a setting with natural lighting and chairs is preferred.

▓ **Meeting customs** – you may host meetings in overseas countries and should seek to be briefed on different customs that might apply.

▓ **Timeliness** – start on time. Attendees don't normally like being kept hanging around.

▓ **Preparation** – the contents and messages should be carefully thought through, and not delivered on the hoof.

▓ **Delivery** – the presentation of information should be structured to match the occasion. For example, regular meetings should be conducted informally, but irregular presentations (say of company announcements) can be more heavily scripted.

▓ **Publishing the agenda** – you should start by saying what you are going to cover. If the meeting is one of a series, you can distribute the full agenda in advance.

▓ **Involving other staff** – you should not assume that the meeting is for personal grandstanding – plan for other staff to speak about issues.

▓ **Taking questions** – questions should always be invited and answered directly – staff can always sense spin or avoidance!

▓ **Repeat messaging** – have no inhibitions about reinforcing key messages, you will be more believable for doing so.

▓ **Action points** – if actions arise from discussions you should commit to following them up and reporting back on progress at subsequent meetings.

The smart leader will closely involve key HR staff in planning and executing regular meetings events – they bear more closely on overall culture and morale than on anything else.

Leaders' measures of success

➤ Staff meetings are held regularly – anything from monthly upwards depending on scale.

➤ Staff meetings are timetabled at least 48 hours in advance.

➤ Action points are noted and dealt with before the next meeting.

Pitfalls

Staff meetings – as any meeting – will fail to achieve their purpose through poor planning or execution.

- **Poor leadership** – a lack of clear and consistent messaging will, in front of a large group, risk suggesting that you do not have a strategy or direction. This can subtly erode any sense of common purpose.

- **Unplanned agenda** – a meeting that is not carefully planned, and where you hop from one subject to the next, will fail to reinforce the messages that are important.

- **Excluded attendees** – staff meetings can become extremely counterproductive when staff are unintentionally excluded, especially if they are remote and are not given the opportunity to dial-in or to have a separate presentation. In these cases the remoteness itself can alienate staff from core messages.

Staff meetings incur some risk. Any leader worth their salt will ask for questions. This can provoke uncomfortable moments where sensitive issues are raised (e.g. salaries) or are simply unexpected. No one can prepare for all questions and there are three golden rules in dealing with them.

- When you know the answer, give it directly and truthfully – staff can always sense evasion.

- When you don't know the answer, say so rather than waffle – and promise to get back to the questioner with the answer at a later point.

- If you know that the answer demands an admission of failure, say so – humility wins friends.

Leaders' checklist

- Be committed to having meetings regularly – understand their role in leadership communication.

■ Use staff meetings to hammer home key messages frequently.

■ Plan the content, delivery and location of meetings carefully.

■ Be sensitive to staff based away from your office and ensure that they do not feel excluded.

■ Always be seen to follow through promised actions.

Collaborating with sister businesses

On many occasions you will need to work with 'sister' businesses or business units in the same organisation for which you have no direct responsibility. Effective everyday leadership demands that you see beyond your silo to represent overall corporate goals.

Frequency – highly unpredictable.
Key participants – mainly peers.
Leadership rating ***

Objective

Synergy is a word used to summon up tired cynical responses – but many of us will so often have been involved in 'synergistic' projects, investments or acquisitions where synergy was easier to state than to achieve. It can take many forms, but is generally best described as the attempt to derive increased value by associating or combining separate activities, competencies or organisation structures. Increased value may arise from increased sales and margin, reduced costs, or both.

Where collaboration of this kind is an apparent opportunity (say, a new business venture), a sharing of knowledge and technology (for example, internal transfer of intellectual property) or a mandated objective (such as a set of post-acquisition targets), there are three essential factors to assess.

■ **Are the desired synergy benefits realistic?** Have they been quantified, and if so, how? Do they represent a set of benefits to be welcomed by customers?

■ **Are the staff involved in such collaboration incentivised towards success?** Are the organisation's goals and objectives aligned in a way that supports the planned collaboration? Or is the collaboration expected to be undertaken on a goodwill basis?

▪ **Have all the barriers to collaboration been assessed?** Are all the impediments to collaboration, invisible as well as visible, fully recognised and factored into deliverability?

*As a leader you will be faced with requirements to collaborate across your organisation outside your immediate area of responsibility. You must balance **effective corporate citizenship** with a realistic assessment of **deliverability**.*

Context

There are many types of multi-divisional organisations. Two examples are:

▪ less fashionable conglomerates where seemingly disparate business activities are melded by a view that common managerial disciplines can generate above-average returns;

▪ businesses orientated to broad sectors (healthcare, infrastructure, construction, information media, education) that identify within their sectors specific segments (often defined as 'vertical markets') which have unique customer characteristics.

In any structure, individual business units will develop their own specific skill sets which they believe are part of their competitive advantage. Very often, however, differences between business sectors belie similarities in customer requirements, technological advances and skill sets. And in an era when organisations value these insights, they will seek to (re)apply these insights across their separate business units rather than repeatedly invest in them separately. Furthermore, in some cases businesses will identify new commercial opportunities that arise *only* because the parent organisation brings together competencies that are currently structured separately.

Challenge

The key challenge is *delivery* – making the collaboration happen. The barriers are frequently substantial.

- **Silos** – if the parent organisation has a history of managing its businesses as a federation, then there will be an enormous residual culture of collegiate separation (rather like a college-based university) that cultivates a pride in separateness and distinctiveness.
- **Culture** – the individual cultures so created will span a wide range of cultural differences and these may be at least as significant as similarities in competence and insight.
- **Targets** – the individual business units will (quite properly) each have their own set of targets, and possibly differently-structured incentive schemes.
- **Focus** – if individual businesses are managed in a focused and customer-orientated manner, they are likely to view inter- or pan-divisional projects as diversionary or peripheral.
- **Communication** – communication systems may be tailored well to heralding the successes of the separate businesses, but less adept at fostering inter-divisional relationships.

Collaboration between separate business units is thus about culture, and it's as simple and as difficult as that:

- **simple** – because it's about attitude;
- **difficult** – because attitudes can be hard to change.

It's also difficult because it's not something that happens by waving a corporate wand – it's an area that requires a consistent and repetitive approach.

Success

The overall business steps that need to be taken are clear but arduous.

- **There must be a mantra for collaboration** – it must be a mantra, and it has to come from the most senior level, i.e. the most senior leadership of a multi-divisional business.
- **The collaboration mantra must be repeated** – it has to become part of the corporate lexicon through endless repetition in every form of discourse within the organisation.
- **The collaboration mantra has to be seen to be real** – areas for collaboration should be identified at group level, and then publicised and prioritised.
- **There must be a parallel values mantra** – statements about collaboration must be supported by a parallel mantra which focuses on the shared values and beliefs that underpin any motivation towards collaboration.
- **Incentive systems must be aligned** – formal incentive systems must be structured to reward priority collaborative areas.
- **Collaboration activities are seen as the norm** – inter-divisional or inter-business unit activities have to become so normal a part of corporate activity that they are the rule rather than the exception.

So when you are required to collaborate across divisions, you should also take some very specific actions.

- **Embody values** – ensure that you embody the corporate values which bring divisions together through your actions and words.
- **Make collaboration the norm** – make it part of your organisation's modus operandi by regarding it as the norm.
- **Coaching** – recognise that an essential part of the added value you bring personally is to coach colleagues to foster collaboration at their respective levels and within their respective functions.
- **Incentivise** – organise incentive systems to reward collaboration – maybe through bonusworthy personal objectives.

This challenge is one of the toughest a leader ever faces. If your business is focused and targeted (with incentive schemes to match), your staff will be dedicated to the goals at hand. Any requirements to work with partner businesses may be seen as irrelevant – and may indeed be tarnished by the cynical perspective that internal collaboration is a replacement for a free(er) choice of external partners or suppliers. Only through your relentless *personalising* of corporate objectives and values will the reality and opportunity of such collaboration be grasped.

Leaders' measures of success

Collaboration is specified in strategic and annual plans.

It is included in key team members' personal objectives.

It is worthy of a bonus.

Pitfalls

Collaboration will backfire when the various criteria I have outlined – shared values, a realistic assessment of benefits, aligned incentive systems and so on – are either not identified or not met. Often, very simply, collaboration fails because sister businesses underestimate the extent to which their legacy cultures are different, and therefore the work that is required to bridge them.

A major source of failure can also be disagreements about 'trading terms', notably how sales and costs are shared between partner businesses. It is easy for this to become an emotional subject and one which obscures an external market opportunity. This is best tackled by focusing on what matters – the opportunity. And also by ensuring that financial arrangements are a facilitator – perhaps by a scheme of double- or triple-counting in which all partner businesses carry all the relevant sales and costs, where duplication is eliminated centrally.

Leaders' checklist

- Do not foster collaboration where it is contrary to your overall organisation or group values – you are wasting your time.

- Where collaboration is a mantra, do it! Support it, talk about it, lead it by organising meetings and conferences, praise others for executing it. If there were ever a case for 'walking the talk' this is it!

- Collaborate selectively – work hard to understand the likely synergies through shared learning and skill sets and focus on those. Like anything else, focus works best!

- Notwithstanding the pursuit of collaboration, praise difference! Sharing skill sets does not mean that businesses are identikits – they will always be different, even subtly, just by virtue of the differences in their leaders. Encourage staff to realise that sharing may also expose them to differences from which they can learn.

- Herald successes publicly – make staff feel good for collaborating and be seen to reward it.

five

Leading performance excellence

If leading your organisation is about ensuring that it is effectively aligned with your Vision and strategy, then leading performance excellence is about delivery. It's about turning concepts into practicalities; visions into realities and objectives into achievements. All in all, it's about what people sometimes call 'walking the talk' – actually doing what you say you're going to do.

Let's face it – no one actually likes failing in work. Everyone likes to have achievable objectives (a clear sense of what is expected of them), a fair opportunity to succeed and appropriate praise when they do so. In truth, most of us welcome criticism when we know in our heart of hearts it is fair, and delivered in a constructive way that allows us to learn and improve. No one likes unachievable goals or unrecognised success.

As leader you start with an enormous asset – teams that want to win, even if they are not aware they can do it, and even if they are unused to being heralded as successes. Your job is to take your team(s) and provide them with the tools to win – to make them stronger where they have weak links; to eliminate unproductive and possibly counterproductive interpersonal difficulties; to set clear, fair and deliverable objectives; and where necessary to allow innovative and challenging ideas and opportunities to take hold.

You are taking your own faith in the certainty of success and transplanting it in others.

This is not an easy task and certainly not plain sailing – not least because some colleagues may be capable of winning but not in your world or with your agenda. You will have tough choices to make, and often unpalatable messages to deliver to colleagues who are not making the mark.

Where you will always win is with the integrity that will be obvious from constant and fair application of principles.

Managing change

Leaders are familiar with the mantra that they are change-managers – your real value as a leader is to make change work and deliver improvement. So you must know how you measure change success.

Frequency – constant.
Key participants – all staff.
Leadership rating ****

Objective

Make no mistake – there is no virtue in change for its own sake, and 'change' should never be regarded as some kind of leader's badge of honour worn to prove machismo. But, equally, be under no illusion – any likely environment you face (public or private sector) will present some combination of circumstances that will force you to change whatever is the status quo.

Your most significant objective is to realise that change is normal, not exceptional, that it is part of the fabric of the way a business operates, not an 'event' that happens once in a while (and hopefully as infrequently as possible). If you think this way then you will know that you must:

- be on the lookout for the need to change at all times;
- prepare your staff for constant change;
- never accept the current 'state of things' as a status quo.

Indeed, such is the pace of change that the most effective leaders are thinking about the next round of changes while implementing the current round.

Regard change as constant – you prepare your staff for constant iterations of change, and help them to regard the **discomfort of change as a new security**.

Context

In managing change, you have to balance and reconcile two opposing forces. The first is the massive range of pressures for change – economic uncertainty, competitor activity, technological innovation, customer demands for lower prices, changes in buying habits from the rise of the internet … This list is very long and very demanding.

At the same time, you have to deliver your team's goals with a group of colleagues for the majority of whom work is their sole source of income, and for whom any impending change may seem to threaten their lives. Too many people derive a sense of achievement and personal dignity from being associated with currently successful approaches, and resent suggestions of change.

Sometimes, prevailing circumstances may not appear to indicate that change is necessary, especially when a business is performing well by its chosen measures of success. It is at this point that the context becomes most dangerous for the leader – the security of success becomes complacent inertia.

You may find the context overwhelming – the sheer range of external market pressures and the sheer difficulty of confronting them with staff make deciding on a course of change seem intimidating.

So to deliver change as a form of security rather than a threat, and to advocate change as a necessity rather than an option, you need one overriding personal quality – it is called *bravery*.

Challenge

Anyone who been through change programmes will know that once a change has been decided (say to organisation structure, process, product range etc.), the next tough challenge is to manage the current business while executing change – what a colleague once described as 'rebuilding a 747 jet while flying it'.

As a *brave* leader you are at once a master strategist, tactician, risk-taker and diplomat:

- **strategist** – because you must have a clear view of how your team and business (unit) needs to develop;
- **tactician** – because you must choose when and how to make change;
- **risk-taker** – because you know that some elements of change may carry a risk for the current business activity;
- **diplomat** – because you have to negotiate this change programme through the possible resistance of colleagues.

It is evident from this range of skills just how complex the management of change can be, and it is in such change that the leader will be most severely tested.

The power of your Vision will require the strongest levels of advocacy and put the greatest strains on the loyalty of your team.

Success

Change is a risk investment. As leader you swap some certainty for uncertainty, and you must be sensitive to some unpredictability of outcome. You cannot insulate yourself from failure, but your *change success* will increase if you follow these steps.

- **Take time** – stand back from the day-to-day stuff to think through the next steps.
- **Ignore the status quo** – imagining a different future requires the current scenario to be rejected, and there is nothing wrong in thinking that.
- **Keep being brave** – imagined futures may seem scary, so you must remind yourself to be brave.
- **Develop allies** – change can be isolating, so you need to recruit allies in your journey progressively so you can share the exploration and bravery!
- **Disregard the naysayers** – as you build allies so you will encounter the naysayers for whom change represents

excessive risk or threat – you must have the courage of your convictions to work round them or without them.

- **Think about the change process early** – a key to successful change management is how it is implemented, so thinking about the *how* of change should be a very early part of your strategy.

- **Structure first, staff next** – never plan the new structure or process for current staff, always make sure the right structure comes first. This is always best for staff in the end as well.

- **Value openness** – when you are describing the reasons for change, you should be as open as possible to avoid any suggestion that there is a hidden agenda.

- **Indulge repetition** – the significance and meaning of planned change will be enhanced through regular description and explanation.

- **Link to Vision and strategy** – you should relate planned changes to your Vision and strategy to demonstrate consistency.

If ever there was an area where the leader 'leads', it is in the area of change. This is where your commitment to your Vision, your power of advocacy, the consistency of your messaging, your bravery and determination and your will to succeed are most rigorously and relentlessly challenged.

Leaders' measures of success

> You worry that you are not confronting required change. In doing so you are being less brave than you should be.

> You discuss change with your HR team.

> For any change plan – of any scale – you define your required outcomes and specifically measure your delivery against them.

Pitfalls

The main enemies of change are fear, inertia and a lack of bravery. If you fall prey to them you will either underestimate the need for change or, having assessed the need for change, lack the will or determination to see it through.

Of course, managing change depends very significantly on experience, and you will gain enormously in your career if early on you work for leaders who are exemplary both in their own change management skills and also in supporting others in theirs. You will also learn the value of a support network – those close colleagues who have the same motivations and perspectives, and who will support you in their own public advocacy.

Process is vital. You will underachieve if you fail to remember – whatever your faith in your convictions – that there are ways and processes to make change effective. Often this can happen because too little time is given to thinking things through.

- Have all the appropriate stakeholders been consulted?
- Have all the risks of a particular change been analysed and detailed?
- What impact will there be on the current business?
- What will be the communication plan, to whom and when?
- Are there particular individuals whose support (or rejection) is critical?
- Have all the legal ramifications been considered?
- Are there any external factors (partners, suppliers, press) that should be taken into account?

The key pitfall in change management, in summary, is a *lack of awareness* – a failure to recognise the need for change and/or poor sensitivity to how process can help in implementation.

Leaders' checklist

- Set aside time to think about change and what the next steps are for your team.

- Don't focus simply on the next set of changes – think two or three steps ahead at a time.

- Make sure you spend as much time as possible with customers, suppliers and partners to ensure that you are as fully exposed as possible to the range of external circumstances driving change.

- Talk about change in your 121s, with your leadership team and wider colleagues – embed it in the daily language of your business life.

- Try always to be as bold as you feel you can be – there is always scope for more, and change is usually more palatable in reality than in the planning!

- When you recruit allies in your change plans, always involve your HR colleagues – they are excellent sounding boards and will ensure that you don't make any serious or damaging faulty steps, especially because any change relating to people's employment may have legal ramifications.

- Remember that implementing change often requires repeated advocacy and that you must be prepared to be challenged.

- You must also be prepared to be disheartened – not everyone will agree with what you are doing and some will put obstacles in the way.

People performance management

Your team are your lifeblood. The right people in the right jobs with the appropriate support, encouragement, feedback and development can deliver superior performance.

Frequency – periodic.
Key participants – direct reports and HR.
Leadership rating ***

Objective

A leader must create the context in which performance is assessed and measured. This is perhaps not as obvious as it sounds – it is about much more than generalised assessments of effectiveness. It demands a clear Vision for an organisation, translated first into a strategy and business plan and subsequently into objectives per business unit or department. These should then be deployed as objectives for individuals.

This cascade is important not simply to align activity, but to set *individual* accountability within an overall framework of *corporate* accountability. The benefit of this is clear – individuals will always be more motivated when they can relate their activities and objectives to their business.

*To this extent, you really are the conductor of the corporate orchestra, directing a score and parts, and **balancing overall cohesion with individual flair**.*

Context

Some key factors that can affect individuals' performance include:

- **personal circumstances** – it is simply unreal to believe that these can be excluded from the work environment, indeed their suppression may well contribute to stress;

- **previously poor relationships** with other leaders, managers and peers which may have contaminated not only the individual but their ability to communicate and demonstrate competence;

- **pigeonholing** – historical, learned assumptions about individuals' strengths and weaknesses which, for whatever reason, may be unrepresentative of their real abilities;

- **cynicism** on the part of individuals who may have been disaffected or discouraged by previous leadership strategies and styles, or by the perceived relentlessness of change;

- **lack of previous feedback**, training and development so that individuals' strengths and weaknesses have never been effectively monitored and developed;

- **poor personal organisation skills** masking relevant competencies;

- **poor interpersonal skills** – this may affect individuals' effectiveness while masking the real contribution they can make;

- **a perceived lack of respect** shown by peers and colleagues contributing to a resentment that can distort performance;

- **stress** arising from any of the above factors – or none of them!

This is not intended to be a definitive list, but sets out to demonstrate how any evaluation of performance requires a sophisticated appreciation of all factors. This does *not* mean that such factors are inevitably regarded as extenuating, only that a clear assessment of action – required next steps – can be more measured and appropriate.

You will also develop antennae to detect poor performance issues – not just by direct observation, but also through explicit and implicit feedback via corporate 'chatter'.

Challenge

You must also consider the appropriateness of your business organisational structure for the demands of its chosen marketplace.

There are many approaches here, but in essence you will attempt to align internal competence with customer demands. This is a major pillar in dealing with performance – an organisation's ability to deliver objectives depends on a clear assessment of the competencies required, and thus the capabilities of staff against those competencies.

So unless you are clear about strategy and objectives, and what competencies are required to deliver them, it is hard to assess performance truly, and impossible to define or evaluate individuals' contributions.

Success

In this regard, I have always found the involvement of HR to be invaluable. HR can have a bad reputation, but that only happens when HR professionals focus on what used to be called 'personnel' – i.e. hiring and firing and record-keeping. When HR takes a broad view, measures the business environmental climate and sees individuals as individuals within a complete context, then it has a major role to play. Indeed, you should actively cultivate a close relationship with your HR professionals because they can provide a 'people prism' through which strategies and decisions can be viewed.

Confronting poor performers with the reality of their under-achievement is tough, not least because many individuals in this position are unaware of their performance issues. And if they are aware then they may create significant defensive barriers to avoid confrontation. You have the primary responsibility as leader of your direct reports to address *their* performance issues, and this can only be done one-to-one.

If you have decided on an exit strategy for a staff member, this should never be implemented without the counsel of HR, first and foremost because any decision to terminate a colleague's employment is, for them, a life-changing event. So you must expect a professional HR representative to challenge the justification of your approach. You must expect that HR will want to ensure that any such decision is taken for defendable reasons. So in the act of dealing with performance, so you will be under scrutiny too.

If endorsed, your exit decision will need to be managed within the prevailing legal framework, which may include guidance on how to run the termination meeting, what can be said, and even the location and timing of such a discussion.

The discussion itself is in one sense the ultimate corporate failure – the admission that recruitment has failed. You should:

- **be direct**, to the point, sensitive and remain aware that in such circumstances reactions are impossible to predict;

- **present a clear follow-up process** (depending on whether the exit is planned to be immediate or deferred) with key opportunities set out for the affected individual to respond, challenge and enter further conversations, notably about financial implications;

- **be aware** that no one will ever thank you for such a decision, but at least they should leave feeling they have been treated fairly, within the law and with dignity.

Alternatively, if you are adopting an improvement approach with a specific individual, you must:

- indicate from the outset, in a discussion, that you want to have a performance meeting with an improvement agenda;

- be prepared to provide evidence of a number of instances of underachievement;

- ask the individual concerned if they have any questions or want to respond immediately;

- set a time for a further discussion.

This should be followed by a separate meeting with relevant staff from HR to enable not only an additional perspective but also to facilitate (if needed) a broader or more reflective conversation. The key output is a mutual agreement about required improvements, and a timetabled agenda for action with agreed and measurable objectives. This should be supported by ongoing feedback about progress, with feedback not restricted solely to formal review points.

To be able to confront identified poor performance demands, as noted above, you need a clear understanding of what is required *from* a role. Attempting to develop a poorly-performing individual against such a standard has no guarantee of success, but the attempt will garner for you what you may come to realise is gold dust – respect for the integrity and courage you display in honesty and good faith.

Leaders' measures of success

➤ All staff have annual appraisals.

➤ Outcomes are recorded, actioned and monitored.

➤ What is the outcome of a regular review with your HR director or manager of performance issues with staff? All issues are aired and being actioned.

Pitfalls

Some people like to rely on instinct and will develop black-or-white views about staff 'fit'. But in the complex dynamic which I am describing in this book, personal performance can be distorted by an array of factors, and I believe that it is your role to understand such nuances. Not least because a leader who is seen to be sensitive to the individual as an individual, and who does not accept received opinions and labels, is more likely to command respect and, in fact, *increase* performance.

This is as thorny an issue to deal with as you will face. It is too easy to assume – even with the power that leadership conveys – that the answer to underperformance is the exit strategy – i.e. the poor performer is summonsed to receive the bad news that 'things are not working out' and despatched under the ambit of the 'compromise agreement' which employment legislation may require. This can be a solution, but this approach can be ultimately self-defeating if it is seen to be typical. To the employee it will give the impression of a 'you are in or you are out' culture, where personal development is sacrificed for short-term expediency. For you, it can represent a get-out which can be used to avoid confronting true leadership challenges.

Leaders' checklist

- Be as clear as you can about the outputs and competencies required for each of your organisational areas to establish standards.

- Engage your HR team in a full analysis of 'fit' against standards, and an identification of weak areas.

- Be absolutely prepared to confront individuals with weak performance, on an evidence basis.

- Regard the process of improvement as an opportunity, not a threat or chore – individuals very rarely don't want to do a good job, or want to face the humiliation of departure, so you have basic motivational drivers on your side.

- Remember that process is an important part of performance improvement, with potential legal pitfalls.

- Recognise that improvement processes of this kind may not come naturally, and that you yourself may require development and support in handling them.

Interpersonal conflict

You shouldn't expect all your staff to 'get on' – indeed some conflict can be constructive. Where you see conflict becoming dysfunctional, you must act, and act quickly.

Frequency – unpredictable.
Key participants – unpredictable.
Leadership rating ***

Objective

A business environment where all colleagues 'get on' with each other, however laudable and potentially enviable, is unlikely to be an environment in which creativity and good business sense flourish if 'getting on' means that issues are ducked and realities not confronted. There is generally no worse environment than the one in which corporate/collective heads are buried in the proverbial sand.

But equally, it is unlikely that a workplace fostered on personal animosity is likely to be one in which the needs of the organisation in its marketplace are met. Of course, there are times when an element of competitiveness between individuals is healthy, especially when the sense of colleagues snapping at your heels sharpens your act. Of course, all organisations are fertile organisms where an element of politics, and the manoeuvring that goes with it, is inevitable.

An organisation will only prosper with individuals who are ambitious, and ambition will lead to energetic rivalry. This rivalry may lead to market-bearing ideas or it may lead to conflict.

*The objective for a leader is how this **competitive energy is harnessed, and how dysfunctional behaviour is eliminated**.*

Context

Organisations have an unerring and innate ability to generate misunderstanding. It is as if, no matter how clear the Vision, how elegant the communication plan, how inclusive the managerial style, some dysfunction is destined to break out.

There is within this characteristic something deeply complex about the employee–employer compact. When an employee joins an organisation, it goes beyond a supplier–client relationship – some element of independence is sacrificed by giving so many waking hours to the employer. An employee's life may be changed by the success or failure of the organisation; emotions may be shaped by the way he or she is respected or disrespected. Once this dependency is established, the employee becomes the organisation's critic, and will likely shower condemnation as much as praise.

It doesn't help that however an organisation nurtures its modernity and its capacity to change, there will always be business units that gather a reputation (fairly or not) for bloody-minded insouciance – the departments that do things 'their way'. Such pinch points enter corporate folklore as standard whipping boys – the targets everyone loves to knock, the ones always thought the worse of, the ones everyone rushes to judge irrespective of evidence.

Finally, into this mix comes a range of alienating interpersonal characteristics:

- failure to listen;
- a tendency to lecture, especially on other colleagues' responsibilities;
- a self-belief that expresses an opinion on every subject;
- failure to communicate because others don't matter;
- failure to communicate because knowledge is power;
- an inability to deliver anything on time;
- excessive absence from the workplace;

- a stubbornness to refuse to back down in the face of incontrovertible evidence;
- the propensity to flog a dead horse;
- the inability to understand the organisational entity in anything other than their own department's terms;
- the belief that business exists for purposes other than for the customer.

Lack of self-awareness would not in itself matter were it not the source of much corporate stress – the frustration that arises from directly suffering poor performance; the bitterness that cannot fathom why 'management' doesn't tackle it; the resentment that in a competitive world someone can 'get away with it'; the sense that it undermines one's own belief in a commitment to excellence.

You should regard this cocktail of emotion and stress as the inevitable by-product of the living organism – which is nothing if it is not about people. You should recognise that:

- where ambition is driving competitiveness, there is a real potential source of competitive advantage;
- that commitment to an organisation is a driver of excellence;
- that however poor a last bastion of underperformance might seem, it can be used as a motivating exemplar of how *not* to operate;
- however uncoupled from corporate goals an individual might seem, the very insecurity that led to dysfunctional behaviour can itself represent the starting point for a transformational change.

Challenge

So your task is to discreetly manage organisation conflict. Rather than seeing it as a unnerving threat (which you might then want to ignore) identify it as a source of improvement – not least because if you are anything as a leader, your role is about fostering permanent improvement as a way of business life.

Indeed, many might say that if there is no conflict there is no life, and that in a bizarre way some conflict is actually a healthy sign.

Success

You will face some broad conflict categories.

- **Where you become aware that a department or team or group is seriously dysfunctional compared with its raison d'être** – this will arise from direct observation or repeated second-hand reports, and you should not take any action based on hearsay. Rumour-based intervention will likely be seen as knee-jerk and unanalytical. Instead, you create a circumstance for a KPI-based review of the group's operational performance. A key judgement will be about the capacity of a team's leader to change and, secondly, the ability of the team to face its own shortcomings.

- **Where you are aware of groups in conflict** – you must raise the issue with the two group leaders together. If the conflict is between their respective teams, then you must agree an approach to bring the issues into the open (perhaps facilitated by HR) with regular reports and feedback on progress.

- **Where there is conflict between two individuals reporting to you** – you should not open a dialogue with them about the source of conflict until you are satisfied that they have attempted to do this themselves. You thus create a culture where disagreements are confronted, but not in a way that others see you as a first port-of-call for conflict resolution that enables them to avoid attempting solutions themselves.

- **Where an individual has a performance issue that is causing conflict** – you are open with them about its existence, why you think it harms the business, and why you think it is in the individual's interest to confront it. You provide evidence-based feedback as soon as possible – not waiting for the annual performance review! You agree an action plan, which is reviewed regularly.

As leader you must always cultivate a business environment in which criticisms can be made freely but are issue- and not personality-based; and in which staff do not express opinions based on the perspective that they can do others' jobs better themselves.

Leaders' measures of success

→ There is a regular audit of conflict issues with HR.

→ Conflict issues are discussed as appropriate during 121s.

→ Known conflict issues are confronted and resolved.

Pitfalls

There are two equal and opposite risks in confronting inter-personal conflict.

- **Doing nothing** – lacking the will or energy to tackle a conflict impeding your business risks undermining your credibility and commitment to your Vision and strategy. Significant conflict is usually easily recognised and if ignored it sends signals that such behaviour is tolerated, or is even acceptable as a norm. It becomes very difficult in these circumstances for you to pursue an achievable agenda of performance excellence.

- **Tackling conflict the wrong way** – confronting issues that are driven largely by personal emotions is always an area in which you must be sensitive to individual difference. Responses to conflict are best moulded and tailored to the individuals concerned. Nothing in this eliminates the need for a clear statement that certain kinds of behaviour are unacceptable – what it means is that success often demands an understanding of the reasons why the specific individual is behaving in the way they are.

The moral here is that tackling conflict requires a demanding blend of courage and adeptness.

Leaders' checklist

- Be alert to signals of conflict – direct or indirect.

- Learn to discriminate between conflict that may represent healthy competitiveness, and conflict that degrades business credibility and performance.

- Never lose sight of the risk that untackled conflict can undermine your organisation's performance.

- Understand that conflict between individuals needs managing differently from conflict between groups.

- Use your HR specialists to assess the significance and impact of conflict, and to determine ways of resolving it.

- Make sure that the leaders of teams where there is unhealthy conflict understand its impact and recognise their responsibility for resolving it.

- Always remember that the source of conflict can be very personal, and that solutions need to reflect the situations and personalities of individuals.

- Be aware that how conflict is tackled sends broader signals to your team about your integrity and resolve.

The difficult interview

This occurs when some tough things need to be said by the leader to one of his or her team, and where the reception to them is unpredictable and possibly hostile.

Frequency – rare.
Key participants – direct reports.
Leadership rating ***

Objective

Sometimes they are unavoidable – the 121 meetings where blunt things need to be said, where you need to convey some negative observations about performance to one of your team. Such interviews may be difficult and lead to conflict:

- **difficult** – because confrontation is usually uncomfortable, almost unavoidably personal, and because interpretations of circumstances may differ;

- **conflictual** – not necessarily an encounter with shouting, aggression, violent disagreement or even tears (though I don't exclude any of these), but because there is a period of disconnection, where the participants disagree fundamentally.

However, these meetings demand *a constructive outcome*, because it is your absolute responsibility to ensure that performance issues are aired, discussed, accepted and tackled.

This is a very difficult area of leadership. Since so much depends on people, you will inevitably be torn between wanting to establish effective and warm relationships, and having to confront uncomfortable realities about possible underperformance. You will be looking to balance empowerment and respect for the individual on one hand, and the overall team's need to succeed on the other. You will be concerned that a conflict arising from blunt conversations might fatally undermine a relationship or damage your larger team's functioning. You may also be plain nervous about face-to-face confrontation.

Three guiding principles will stand you in good stead.

- Trust your judgement and, if needs be, support it by sounding out peers or HR colleagues.
- Be aware that poor performance that is unaddressed is poor performance *compounded* – further deterioration is a major risk, which in due course will undermine the reputation of the leader's own judgement.
- It is in your colleagues' interests that issues are addressed, even if they don't like hearing what you have to say – in the long run they will recognise your integrity and respect you for enabling their self-improvement.

No matter how difficult it may appear, you must confront any of your team head-on, face-to-face, if there are performance issues – **your credibility and integrity rest on it**.

Context

The initial assessment must first be whether or not an issue is serious enough to merit any action. Here you depend very much on your instincts and experience. You need to stand back from any emotion that others may have expressed, and reassess the reactions you have had.

Your assessment needs to take into account the severity of the case. Is the problem sporadic or consistent? Is the issue part of the process of relationships being established (the so-called 'storming' phase) and consequently may blow itself out? If so, the best course of action is to do nothing.

If you come to the conclusion that the issue must be confronted, you should consider if your HR director/manager might provide a more effective solution. In certain cases, the relative independence of an HR director may allow them to have a discussion that feels less confrontational to your colleague – though this needs to be balanced against the impression of seriousness that will be conveyed if you yourself take up the issue.

The point is that confronting issues, while a necessity, should be done in a considered, measured and unemotional manner.

Challenge

I do not subscribe to the view that certain levels of staff are in any way above such considerations, and that the leader should adopt a take-it-or-leave-it approach. Such an attitude to behaviour and performance is complacent, evasive and not even in the best interests of staff.

We all benefit from constructive feedback that can inform not only our current performance but also our career path. In turn, your staff need to know that you *will* confront issues, that you approach them with fairness and integrity and that you are driven solely by a desire to maximise their and the organisation's performance. They may not thank you for it, but they will respect you.

Success

If you reach the conclusion that you are going to tackle the issue yourself, you must arrange to see the colleague involved – and make a fixed appointment to ensure that meeting is not allowed to happen by chance. As this is not a formal disciplinary meeting, no advance warning of the subject is necessary or desirable. The meeting should be organised in such a way that it is not disturbed.

In these circumstances nothing is to be gained by talking round the issue – you need to get to the point – but it is vital that you follow some ground rules in your approach and what you say.

- **Preparation** – enter the discussion with notes about what you want to say.

- **Starting** – say that you want to discuss a performance issue on an informal basis.

- **Set the context** – make it clear that the purpose is an open and fair discussion and that you have not arrived at any predetermined conclusions.

- **State the role of HR** – inform your colleague that you have discussed the issue with the HR director/manager to convey that you have taken advice on its seriousness and also to demonstrate that you want to deal with the issue in the most appropriate manner.

- **The issue** – state the issue and describe what you think it is and the impact it is having.

- **Give examples** – support your analysis with some specific examples, which you cite as demonstrating the reality of the problem.

- **Give more examples** – retain further examples for later in the conversation.

- **Provoke a discussion** – ask your colleague to comment.

This is the point where the nub of the conversation is reached – does your colleague's reaction convey any sense that they recognise the issue? They may attempt to avoid the issue by raising issues about other people's personalities, performance or behaviour. You need to be firm in asserting that the conversation is *not* about others. You may then give further examples and try to engage your colleague in changing their self-perception.

The way such conversations develop is highly unpredictable, not least because most of us don't like being challenged, and when we are we tend to react emotionally or defensively. The key here is to stick to your guns – to lay out the issues with clear examples, to allow your colleague to challenge and respond, yet ensure that the issue is not lost.

An overriding principle in such discussions must always be a focus on *behaviour* and not *personality*. Generally speaking, you should never attempt to challenge or change an individual's personality – you should respect colleagues for what they are. Your interest as a leader is in how they behave and how their behaviour interacts with and affects others – this is the touch point with business performance. Thus such 'conflict' discussions remain focused not on who people are, but on how their actions are perceived by and affect others.

No conversation of this kind works unless there is a follow-up, which can take a number of forms depending on the responsiveness of the colleague in question, but these are likely to include:

- agreeing to a period of reflection, and a further meeting to discuss the issues again;
- involving the HR representative in a separate conversation with the colleague to provide a less emotionally-charged perspective from a people-professional;
- agreeing that the issue will be monitored and that ongoing feedback will be given;
- if necessary setting specific performance goals, with a future review.

Once you have decided to have the 'difficult' conversation, as much is gained in the manner you conduct it as in the content of the conversation itself.

Leaders' measures of success

→ All the points noted in advance of the difficult interviews were covered.

→ Was the colleague prepared to be constructive – i.e. was there an open conversation about the issues raised?

→ A series of follow-up actions was agreed.

Pitfalls

What is most likely to backfire in a difficult conversation is an approach that has been poorly thought through. This is no occasion for off-the-cuff commentary. To the contrary, precisely because such a conversation is so personal, it needs the most careful and detailed preparation. So the conversation may backfire if:

■ the context has not been fully evaluated;

■ you have allowed your own emotional response to dictate the preparation;

■ the issue is presented in emotional rather than business terms;

■ the issue is presented as one of personality rather than behaviour;

■ you allow an emotional reaction to provoke an emotional one in yourself;

■ the issue is not described with substantive evidence;

■ there is inadequate time provided for the discussion, which gets truncated;

■ you send signals that you are not focused on the conversation;

■ there is no suggestion that there will be further feedback or discussion.

Such a conversation – however difficult – can reap rich rewards in the performance improvement it can provoke. But if it backfires through careless preparation or thoughtless management, the legacy can be damaging and long-lasting.

Leaders' checklist

■ Be sure to evaluate the context, and don't rush to hasty judgements – some issues may be transitional and will blow themselves out.

■ When you perceive a difficult issue then it requires a one-to-one approach – be sure that you have clear evidence and examples.

■ Be sure that you have a clear process in mind – do not allow vagueness or lack of preparation to be seen to diminish the importance of the issue.

▦ Do not allow emotional reactions to your comments to provoke an emotional response – be seen to stay cool.

▦ Involve HR if you feel this would facilitate the process of a colleague accepting that there are issues to be confronted.

▦ At all times be clear that the challenge is in your colleague's interests and that you are doing it to help.

▦ Have clear, timetabled and measurable follow-up.

Objectives and incentives

Employees' performance is always more likely to be optimised when they have clear objectives and, if possible, linked financial incentives.

Frequency – annual with mid-year review.
Key participants – at least direct reports.
Leadership rating ***

Objective

In leading an organisation with a clear Vision and strategy, you must ensure that:

- the strategies and actions of your teams and individuals are aligned to overall goals so that the organisation gives itself the best chance of success;
- individuals have clear performance targets and rewards so that they can share in success, their strengths can be enhanced and their weaknesses addressed.

Setting integrated objectives and incentives is not a formulaic approach designed to satisfy only the needs of the HR department. It really is true that organisations can be significantly undermined when teams and individuals have goals that are inconsistent with their organisation's overall ambitions. By having a clear and documented structure for objectives and related incentives, you ensure that the power of your Vision and strategy – however well communicated – is translated into the detail of daily behaviour because this is often where a difference is made.

*You should not be satisfied unless and until you are sure that your overall strategies are reflected in what teams and individuals are actually asked to do, and are rewarded for doing, on **a day-to-day basis**.*

Context

Post-credit crunch bank bonuses have been the subject of huge attention, not least because of the widespread perception that banks reward failure. While the bank bonus issue is actually related to an extremely small number of people in the overall workforce, it does highlight a very real challenge about the relationship between performance and reward.

The leader of any organisation will confront the following questions.

- What part of a team member's role is core – i.e. part of the basic 'job description' – and what they are fundamentally paid for?
- What objectives should be added on a regular basis (usually annually) above and beyond the core role?
- What is the role of these additional objectives in assessing the individual's performance?
- How much should the individual be paid for their core role?
- How much *more* should the individual be paid for performance above the core role?
- To what extent should the individual's incentives be linked to personal, to team and to overall organisation performance objectives and performance?

Many of the answers to these questions are driven by *cultural context* – broader challenges about the nature of the organisation, its ethos and the business sector within which it operates.

Challenge

It is easy as a leader to overlook the significance of objectives and incentives. You may think that:

- because the overall objectives of the business are well known, individual objectives are obvious;

- because incentive payments for many staff may be small in absolute terms, they are of little value.

This overlooks the reality that:

- without clear objectives, staff will often do what they prefer rather than what is necessary, and become unfocused;
- incentive payments that look small to one person may be very meaningful to families with tight finances.

You must be seen to take these issues seriously, and to ensure that objectives and incentives are set in a clear and timely manner.

Success

You will be setting objectives and incentives within a overall framework determined by your organisation and will be unlikely to have free rein to do anything you want. You are also likely to be obliged to manage the objective and incentive process with your HR team to ensure consistency and conformance with overall policies. It is a detailed and arduous process if managed appropriately.

Objectives

- **Annual objectives** – these should be published as near as possible to the start of the team's financial year. Objectives are always less effective if they are made known too long after the year has started.
- **Team objective setting** – these should be presented formally by you to your team and to wider colleagues through presentations (WebEx where needed) and be supported by clear information circulated to staff by e-mail or published on the organisation's intranet. You should also reiterate the objectives relentlessly during the year, including *why* they have been chosen and how they link to your overall Vision and strategy.

- **Direct reports** – you should arrange meetings with all your direct reports (and ensure that they do the same with theirs) to discuss personal objectives.

- **Individual objective setting** – it is usually more effective to ask someone to propose their objectives than to impose them, so the personal objective phase will likely have three stages:

  - you suggest in advance of a meeting that your direct report proposes objectives for the year;

  - a meeting is held to review the proposed objectives;

  - the finalised objectives are agreed in a further meeting or by e-mail exchange depending on the level of agreement.

- **Focused objectives** – objectives are always best kept limited (by definition they have to be focused to be achievable) and no more than five or six in a given period is advisable.

- **Mid-year review** – after objectives are agreed, a mid-year review point should be set to assess progress.

- **Recording objectives** – nowadays many organisations use electronic systems to record, amalgamate and monitor objectives and progress (this enables the leader to see who has not set objectives).

Incentives

- **Incentive plans** – should be issued as early as possible in the financial year so that recipients have maximum opportunity to deliver success against them.

- **Incentive details** – the incentive arrangements should clearly set out the balance between company, team and individual performance.

- **Personal objectives** – where there is a personal element, they should refer to the agreed personal objectives (above).

- **Incentive criteria** – any criteria that affect entitlement to incentives should be stated clearly because they can lead to misunderstanding. For example:

- is there an override that no payments are made for personal performance if the organisation fails to meet certain financial targets?
- does the employee have to be in employment on a certain date to receive a bonus? This is usually the case, and sometimes the date falls *after* the end of the bonus period.

- **Recording bonus plans** – bonus plans should be signed and recorded formally.

- **Progress reports** – you should not be embarrassed about reporting back to staff during the year about progress against bonus milestones where they affect the whole team – this is not a subject attracting silence for 12 months.

For both objectives and incentives, you must also ensure that where these are being set by your direct reports, they too are following all the guidelines applied by the organisation and that their implementation processes are overseen by the HR team.

What is evident is that successful objective and incentive schemes rely, above all else, on attention to detail.

Leaders' measures of success

- → All direct reports have agreed objective and incentive plans.
- → When the plans were issued in the financial year.
- → Mid-year review dates were set.

Pitfalls

Very often a simple acronym is used to describe objectives – **SMART**.

- **S**pecific – objectives should specify what they want to achieve.
- **M**easurable – you should be able to measure whether you are meeting the objectives or not.

- Achievable – are the objectives you set, achievable and attainable?

- Realistic – can you realistically achieve the objectives with the resources you have?

- Time – when do you want to achieve the set objectives?

That this summary is so familiar does not lessen its significance – 'objectives' will fail in their own objective of managing and aligning performance if they are not useable. By extension, if objectives give an inaccurate guide for performance, then incentive programmes will themselves become ineffective.

Leaders' checklist

- Remember that objectives and incentives are not worthy of the name if they are not linked to the overall Vision and strategy.

- Take objective-setting seriously – as leader you should regard it as an integral and not peripheral part of performance management.

- Manage the objective-setting process with your team in a structured manner with at least one mid-year progress review.

- Regard objectives and incentives as part of the overall performance management system and ensure they are linked to specific corporate goals.

- Ensure that objectives follow SMART principles.

- Ensure that incentives are specifically linked to corporate and personal goals and do not deliver something for nothing.

SIX

Customers: leading you

Leadership is really tough – there's always so much to think about, so many issues to balance, so many challenges to doing the right thing. However much is planned, there will *always* be the unexpected. But what you can always be certain about is that your business depends on your customers – without them there is no business for you to think about.

Your role as leader is to ensure that your team does not regard customers as a group 'out there', individuals or entities that they sell 'to'. Your big task is to bring customers on the inside – to create a business culture whose very nature and whose every decision is informed by the perspective of what the customer wants.

This is not about 'knowing the customer', if that means understanding how to manage them; it not about providing excellent service (important though that is) and it is not about regular surveys of what your customers think about you.

What it *is* about is opening the physical and mental doors to your business and forming partnerships so that customers shape your activities from their core outwards – it is about seeing customers as a key part of your business development process, not a recipient of it; it is about strategic rather than transactional relationships. It is about knowing how much you can learn from customers.

Most of all it is about humility. It is about recognising that leadership of your business exists outside the potentially exclusive and excluding world you inhabit with your leadership team. In the best cases it lies within, and should be shared with, your most valued customers – they lead you to where your leadership alone would not have trodden.

The importance of the customer

It is the customer who shapes a business, whose needs are met. In the end, if there's no customer, there's no business. The leader must ensure that all the staff put the customer first in their priorities.

Frequency – constant iteration.
Key participants – all staff.
Leadership rating ****

Objective

It is a simple and obvious truth that without customers a business doesn't exist. As a leader you must set yourself the objective of ensuring that across your team and operations, it is the customer's perspective that is applied in decision-making and planning. This will inevitably mean reaching outside the organisational structure and seeing customers as partners, not simply recipients of goods and services.

This objective will encompass five broad but key areas:

- what products and services customers want;
- how much they are prepared to pay;
- how the business sells and markets itself;
- how the business communicates;
- how the business manages service.

*Your role is to ensure that your team have the awareness and humility so that at all times they see themselves **through the customer's prism**.*

Context

Seeing the customer as 'prime' is part of a broader set of cultural statements you make to ensure that your organisation operates in a market-sensitive manner. These include, notably:

- the role of *all* staff in implementing the Vision and strategy;
- how *all* staff affect sales;
- how *all* staff 'market' the business;
- how customer service is a value for *all*, not a department;
- the importance of process in *all* teams to delivering carefully-managed customer interfaces.

The central goals are:

- to bind an organisation together in a common purpose where all staff know that together they affect performance;
- to prevent fragmentation of effort where the customer is seen to belong to certain departments only.

Challenge

The simple truth of the 'importance of the customer' can become overlooked in the challenges of daily business:

- the sheer pressure of events and tasks;
- the absence of discussions about or references to customers by senior managers;
- the cycle of weekly, monthly, quarterly and annual processes, which can becomes ends in themselves;
- the actions of competitors and vendors, which can very rapidly affect day-to-day perceptions of the market;
- a focus on managing systems and processes, which are by definition largely internal;
- the effect of working in a close-knit 'team', which again by definition is internal and excludes customers.

The response to these challenges is to make the customer part of the organisation's lexicon – *the* reference point for planning strategic development.

Success

To be an effective leader championing the customer you have to be relentless in bringing the customer into focus across your team:

- **Talk about the customer** – the customer should be referred to in all team meetings, update e-mails and presentations so they are seen to matter.
- **Team meeting agendas** – time should be allocated to customer issues (separate from sales) at all team meetings.
- **Meet customers yourself** – this shows you mean it!
- **Encourage others to meet customers** – as many staff as possible should be encouraged to do this.
- **Learn about the customer** – meeting customers should be used as way of learning about how their lives, markets or businesses are changing.
- **Customer feedback collection** – however collected (meetings, e-mails, phone calls) this should be collated so there is a precise record of what is being said about the business.
- **Customer feedback circulation** – so that as many staff as possible are aware of what customers are saying.
- **Customer satisfaction measures** – informal feedback should be set alongside formal measures of satisfaction collected through planned surveys.
- **Meet new customers** – try to find ways to meet people who might be potential customers, and identify what would make them switch.
- **Meet customer groups** – some customers form groups to represent common issues and you should meet these to understand trends.
- **Focus groups** – use these with customers wherever it makes sense.
- **Strategic planning** – define and develop customer strategies in strategic and annual plans.

■ **Evangelise customers to 'non-customer' groups** – make a special point of discussing customers with groups who often historically don't see themselves as having anything to do with sales or service (IT, finance, facilities).

If ever there was an area requiring dedication and commitment – even evangelism – this is one. Unless and until you relentlessly 'talk' customers to all staff, unless and until they see and hear you are serious, they won't be.

Leaders' measures of success

➤ Customers are discussed.

➤ Customers are met.

➤ Customers' opinions are collated and published.

Pitfalls

The risk of any mantra – which can seem like an obsession – is that it is disconnected from your team's working experience. Any one of them might say:

■ we don't do the market research;

■ we don't design the product;

■ we don't make the sales calls;

■ we don't take the service calls/complaints;

■ we don't design or write the marketing;

■ we don't manage customer credit;

■ we never meet or talk to customers.

And some of them may indeed do none of these. The answer is:

■ to implement the actions described above so fully that they cannot but feel connected to customer experiences;

■ to ask any doubters to consider – and analyse – what they do that *does* touch customers and to expand their customer insight from that (narrower) point.

Leaders' checklist

■ Talk relentlessly about the customer – don't be afraid to do so!

■ Talk to all the members of your team – there is no one who does not have customer impact.

■ Keep making the point that the customer belongs to everyone and to no single department.

■ Lay plans so that as many people as possible actually meet customers.

■ Ensure that customer feedback is collated and circulated as widely as possible.

■ Identify, collect and publish measures of customer satisfaction.

The customer journey 1: customer experience

Even as you instil the 'importance of the customer', you must embark on a detailed understanding of those points of 'engagement' with the customer to ensure that they deliver to the customer's expectations.

Frequency – regular reviews.
Key participants – all staff without exception.
Leadership rating **

Objective

As leader you are the ultimate champion of the customer. No one else can be, and if the organisation sees that the leader puts the customer in lower than first place, it will ultimately follow this lead – and the customer will be repeatedly and increasingly disappointed. Some part of this 'importance of the customer' is, of course, ensuring that products and services meet customer needs. But the limitation of this most obvious of business requirements is that it overlooks the entire process of *engagement* – all those points of contact where the customer 'meets' the supplier. Here the risk is that the organisation is so absorbed in its product creation that it overlooks how this may be a very limited part of its customer engagement process.

Whether you run a new business charting its first foray into a new market or are the leader of an established business, you must stand back and evangelise the *customer journey* – the entire process of understanding those areas which I call the 'touch points' where you engage the customer before, during or after a sale. This is a potentially complex and extended analytical process – it may challenge many assumptions, expose tensions between functions and undermine what the business believes are its unique selling points.

The ultimate benefit, however, is a sharper understanding of how the customer sees the business, how your competition operates and a clear focus on how your business can derive competitive advantage.

The customer journey *forces a business* **to turn a mirror on itself** *– to see itself, good and bad, as others do.*

Context

Organisations can all too easily lose sight of what it is like for customers to engage with them. There is a variety of reasons.

- Internal processes and systems that often represent history and legacy rather than future intent.
- Increasingly automated customer interfaces which are specifically designed to reduce customer contact time.
- Continual pressures on cost, driving a culture of doing less rather than more.
- Overidentification with products for their own sake, rather than the benefits customers seek.
- Incentive systems that may not include customer-facing measures.

Maintaining the centrality of the customer is a relentless battle against 'internalism', short-sightedness and expediency.

Challenge

It is often very easy to confuse the internal and external identities of an organisation. At worst this leads an organisation to describe and label itself to customers in terms that reflect more on its internal structural nuances than their needs. In the same way, if leaders are not careful, they can see their customers – and their customers' experiences – in the organisational terms that they must necessarily create to manage their business pragmatically – operations, sales, marketing, credit control and so on.

The risk here is that customer-facing strategies are either set primarily within 'product' or 'customer service' functions, or more broadly department by department. Such organisational differences, while they matter a great deal within organisations – they are the key markers for all-important internal identities – cannot, and should not, be taken to reflect how a customer sees the supplier.

Success

There are several steps in the *customer journey* process, led by you.

- **Describing what the 'customer journey' is** – you explain to your team the nature of the process and why it needs to be undertaken.

- **Appointing a customer champion** – this is the person who will lead the process and argue the case of the customer. This is likely to be (though it does not need to be) someone from the sales function, provided they are objective enough not to champion established hobby-horses.

- **Establishing a team to review the customer journey** – this will involve representatives of all core functions, not least because of the continual emphasis that *marketing is everyone* and that no one is divorced from customer engagement.

- **Setting the brief** – the goal is to review, end-to-end, the ways in which customers 'meet' the business in order to ensure that these contact points connect seamlessly and deliver desired competitive advantages. This analysis should include comparisons with key competitors.

- **Including customers** – you insist that customers themselves are included in the process (exactly how and when requires careful analysis). Through this involvement, the review team is fully exposed to the reality of how the organisation is viewed externally.

- **Setting objectives** – you determine required outcomes. This does not need to include an analysis structure because the process of investigating the customer journey will itself drive this.

The outcome should be:

- a documented – probably narrative, possibly diagrammatic – description of all customer touch points;
- a clear analysis of competitor behaviour in each area;
- an objective assessment of your organisation's comparative performance;
- recommendations for action and improvement in each area;
- regular implementation reviews.

By forcing input from all functional teams, you will have reinforced the importance of the customer to every department, and also ensured that multi-dimensional issues receive a multi-dimensional analysis. This is absolutely critical because it is often the lack of a multi-dimensional approach that means the customer loses out.

Leaders' measures of success

The customer journey review gives a complete analysis of all customer touch points.

There is a documented and timetabled follow-up action plan. Is it being reviewed regularly?

The organisation has agreed measures of customer satisfaction. What is their trend after the implementation of the customer journey process?

Pitfalls

If you are the customer's ultimate champion, then the customer journey cannot be a one-time process. It has to become a permanent way of thinking, a mantra within the organisation's corporate language. If not, then the process will be seen to be an event or fad.

The centrality of the customer journey can be reinforced by stipulating, for example, that the 'customer' is a standing item on regular management meeting agendas (not, you will notice, 'customer service'). In addition, you can request regular – say quarterly – customer journey updates or re-reviews. Finally, you should be prepared to articulate the significance of the customer journey to all your staff and commercial partners.

There might be a view that a customer journey evaluation sounds like business process re-engineering (BPR) by another name, but in my experience BPR tends to be focused on internal processes and associated costs. I would strongly advocate that any such re-engineering processes are always done with the customer journey review to hand, so that BPR outcomes are consistent with customer needs. How many damaging process changes (like excessively outsourced and automated call centres) would have been avoided if the customer journey had been in place?

Leaders' checklist

- Be a relentless champion of the customer and customer needs. Endeavour to infuse this approach into all discourse and all subjects, and to demonstrate by example that it is the customer not the organisation that leads your approach.

- Introduce the customer journey concept as only one of a number of methodologies to remain customer-facing.

- Do not accept that either sales or customer service departments alone are in some way the proprietors of the customer – urge all departments to see themselves as part of the never-ending battle to meet customer needs.

- Use the customer journey process regularly (through updates) not only to reinforce your customer-first message, but also to ensure that the organisation confronts the *changing* needs of customers.

- Be unafraid to include customers themselves in aspects of this process – indeed welcome, encourage and insist on it.

The customer journey 2: technology journey

However thoroughly a business reviews its customer touch points, it also needs to be sure that its technology strategy is aligned to the customer.

Frequency – periodic reviews.
Key participants – all customer-facing staff.
Leadership rating **

Objective

No business today operates without even the most rudimentary PC-based technology. Increasingly technology underpins nearly every customer interface. Consider even a limited list:

- online ordering and e-mail confirmations;
- speech-recognition telephone ordering;
- SMS-based purchasing;
- credit card and Paypal payment systems;
- web-based customer service;
- online information resources – including 'frequently asked questions';
- electronic monitoring of delivery logistics, including handheld electronic receipt/signature technology;
- call-centre queue management systems with scripted 'Touch button 1' routines.

As a leader you need to assess clearly that the implementation of such technologies – often seen as so normal that they are a prerequisite – actually supports your organisation's Vision of the customer journey. You need to verify, in particular, that technology does not become a barrier between your business and its customers.

*You must ensure that **technology enables a successful customer journey, not frustrates it**.*

Context

Customer-interfacing technologies of the type noted above are widely available and widely implemented. Most of us would recognise their value in:

■ **reducing cost and increasing efficiency** – there is a widespread acceptance that customer-facing technologies can automate previously human manual-tasks and also process data (and thus provide service) more quickly (for example, paying online rather than reading out credit card details over the phone);

■ **improving the customer experience** – many customers like the control that online shopping provides; they determine where and when they shop, away from the physical and opening-hours constraints of bricks-and-mortar outlets because most online stores operate 24/7/365;

■ **increasing choice** – many customer-facing technologies have widened the availability of goods to consumers (for example, the range of books sold at amazon.com);

■ **increasing knowledge** – many consumers now know more about what they are evaluating (for example, the 3-D imagery often used by estate agents to showcase properties);

■ **increasing purchasing power** – many customers like the greater control technology can afford (for example, personally selecting online their precise seat location in a theatre).

These are essentially generic benefits that work in the specific ways I have indicated. Your challenge in this context is to ensure that your business identifies the specific and not the generic benefits:

Challenge

Technology is now so ubiquitous that gone are (or should be) the days of the 'IT' department. Leaders recognise that technology is not a department or a function but a tool for *all* teams. They understand that there are at least six areas of customer-interacting technology that need to be assessed and understood separately.

- **Corporate infrastructure** – while this may primarily affect internal networks and capabilities, certain elements will affect customer experiences; for example the management of bandwidth will affect the ease of use of websites.

- **Online ordering systems (e-commerce)** – some key choices may have to be made here; for example the currencies and credit cards that are accepted, whether or not the organisation supports systems like PayPal.

- **Online advertising** – at the core is the organisation's websites, and just because they are 'there' doesn't mean they can be used. Some sites, for example, require the user to download the latest version of Flash to be viewable and this may impinge on the customer's experience, or completely deter them.

- **Online marketing** – the use of social networking sites (SNS), supported by search engine optimisation (SEO) is an increasingly critical aspect of online marketing, requiring specific skill sets about marketers.

- **Technology-based products** – a vast area, of course, critical down to the level of product compatibility (or not) with other systems; for example the PC specifications required to run a software product.

- **Call-centre management** – organisations operating call centres invest enormously in automated queue management systems. The impact of these is of huge significance to customer experience, especially as their front-ends usually involve numeric choice systems.

You will not go wrong in understanding the value of technology in these areas if you remember to see them through the eyes of the customer.

Success

In essence, you should review technology as a separate but subsequent process from what was described in *Customer Journey 1*. The three simple steps are:

- **complete customer journey 1** – this is essentially a non-technical perspective because it is mapping customer touch points;
- **overlay customer journey 2** – this creates a 'technology journey' which describes the primary customer journey in terms of technology;
- **assess the risks and vulnerabilities of the technology journey** – this means re-reviewing how the customer 'meets' the organisation through its technology and what the actual impacts are.

There are some basic questions that should inform such a review.

- Does the technology deliver what we say it does and what the customer wants?
- How much does the organisation's use of technology demand changes in behaviour from the customer?
- How much are customers themselves being expected to meet certain technology standards?
- What is it that the technology is *not* doing?

There is no embarrassment in asking such *basic* questions – these are often the ones which are overlooked in the rush to 'technologise'.

Leaders' measures of success

→ There is a technology journey mapped to the primary customer journey.

→ It identifies the specific ways customers interface with technology.

→ There is a risk assessment for each interface.

Pitfalls

Reviewing your technology journey is a *must*. You *must* see your organisation's technology through your customers' eyes. The greatest risk is being fobbed off by siren voices who argue that:

- technology should be reviewed by the technology people;
- the technology is too diverse and complex to be reviewed;
- there are many different technologies, some of which lack interoperability, so an integrated review is impossible;
- there are many legacy systems that limit what is achievable;
- customers don't see their interactions as any form of 'technology journey' so the effort is pointless anyway.

You have to ignore being led by these observations to the greatest possible pitfall – *doing nothing*.

Leaders' checklist

- Be alert to the extent that technology suffuses all your business activities, but don't let it be run by technologists!

- Ensure that your people-development plans adequately identify the need for technological competence across all teams.

- Make your teams understand why you need a separate technology journey review – to verify that your customer promises are *actually* being delivered.

- See what technology does from the customers' viewpoint and always maintain that perspective.

Sell! Sell! Sell!

Selling is an organisation's lifeblood. By focusing on 'Sell! Sell! Sell!' you show that selling is part of everyone's role.

Frequency – forever.
Key participants – everyone.
Leadership rating ***

Objective

It is all to easy to think that 'sales' belongs to the 'sales department', that anyone who does not have 'sales' in their job title or job description is not 'in' sales. This kind of compartmentalised view allows people to distance themselves from sales issues, especially if sales are not at the level the organisation is seeking.

You have a straightforward task – you think and believe in 'Sell! Sell! Sell!' and need your team to realise that:

- without sales the business is nothing;
- the whole team or organisation is accountable for sales;
- 'sales' is the name of a team that is likely to have primary contact with the customer, but not a description of accountability;
- every function has an impact on sales, whether you realise it or not;
- all teams – whatever they are called – should expect to be involved in and contribute to discussions on sales.

You may have an additional challenge depending on the nature of your organisation. Some organisations don't talk openly about sales with all their staff – not because sales are viewed as 'departmental', but because there is a general reluctance or embarrassment to raise the issue in public. Your role is to ensure that sales *are* discussed, everywhere and with everyone.

You are chief sales officer – *unless you are seen and heard to talk about sales, unless you advocate 'Sell! Sell! Sell!', the organisation will not realise that* **sales is the responsibility of everyone.**

Context

Probably all of us have been in organisations where there is a structural fragmentation between the people who conceive, make, market, sell and support a product or service. Each of these broad functions contains specifically-qualified professionals who first and foremost identify with their given specialisms. And since there is a professional area called 'sales', the majority of staff will see sales as belonging in that 'box'.

Businesses have increasingly complex interactions with customers, driven especially by technology – by products which are themselves technology-based, and by sales and support systems that are based on technology. The complexity of the engagement makes it impossible for sales to be an isolated function, in the same way that no one should now advocate an 'IT' department that owns technology.

As leader you need to pluralise responsibilities in an environment where knowledge and specialisms are increasingly shared. Who could now operate a design studio or a web service without individuals who are both creative and technology-wise?

Thus in sales:

- the sales 'department' manages the customer relationship;
- the actual sales team is the whole business.

Challenge

Sell! Sell! Sell! becomes a mantra by which you evangelise the importance of sales and everyone's participation in sales as *the cause* in the organisation. You will face the sternest of resistance to this endeavour in some cases:

- some staff in the 'sales' team will believe that sales is for them and will fear the intervention of outsiders;
- some non-sales staff will believe that 'sales' is nothing to do with them;
- some team members will buy into the concept, but will argue that they have little time to 'think sales' given the load of their existing responsibilities;
- some people will buy into the concept, but not see how they can affect sales, especially if they work in a very different area;
- some staff may only respond if such an approach is tied to specific monetary incentives;
- some may think *Sell! Sell! Sell!* is nothing but grandstanding.

Like all mantras, where the leader has faith, commitment and resolve, so the doubters can be won over.

Success

You will embark on *Sell! Sell! Sell!* as an endeavour for your whole tenure and not as a single event. You can embed sales in the whole organisation if you:

- **talk about sales in every public presentation** – making it clear, very literally, that sales is on your mind;
- **put sales at the top of your team meetings agenda** – emphasising its centrality to the organisation's existence;
- **meet key customers** – reiterating the message that sales is for everyone;
- **travel with sales staff on the road** – to understand what the experience with customers is like for staff at the coal-face;
- **listen to customer sales or service calls on the telephone** – this further enables you to hear real customers describing their experiences with the organisation;
- **conduct sales team workshops** – you facilitate detailed

discussions with the sales team to understand in detail what impediments to making sales they see in the organisation;

■ **insist that all your direct reports meet customers and listen to call-centre calls (if relevant)** – this again reinforces the 'sales is for everyone' message, and exposes all senior staff to actual customers;

■ **publicise sales efforts in regular e-mail communications** – if you talk about sales performance in all kinds of regular staff communications, you make it clear that sales is a never-ending purpose;

■ **ensure that sales performance is displayed** – sales data should be highlighted by electronic scoreboards or wall charts posted in key locations so that all staff see actual data;

■ **review 'sales impacts' with all departments** – you work with every team to assess how they contribute directly or indirectly to sales efforts;

■ **conduct periodic Sell! Sell! Sell! campaigns** – where the business faces particular sales challenges, include all staff in sales campaigns so they are not seen as belonging to the 'sales' team;

■ **create organisation-wide incentives for sales campaigns** – to seek to spread rewards and incentives;

■ **launch organisation-wide 'sales idea' programmes** – periodically invite all staff – whatever their function – to contribute ideas about generating sales.

You have many rich seams you can tap to generate enthusiasm for sales across your whole work community. You really can make all staff believe they affect sales. But as the breadth of the activities noted above shows, this requires action on many fronts at once.

Leaders' measures of success

→ You talk sales.

→ Sales are in everyone's objectives and incentives, where relevant.

→ Sales targets and performance are made visible in the organisation.

Pitfalls

An approach like *Sell! Sell! Sell!* requires a relentless and fearlessly dedicated approach. This will be undermined if:

- **the leader lets go** – you fail to see the approach through and allow yourself to lose focus on sales as the organisation's lifeblood;
- **the leader lacks support** – you fail to persuade your direct reports of the overriding significance of sales;
- **the leader fails to communicate clearly to staff** – and there is a widespread belief that, after all, sales really is for the sales team.

How do you avoid these pitfalls? Pretty much by keeping going whatever the response, whatever the difficulties. Like all the mantras described in this book, there is little room for self-doubt – where this is creeping in, you need to find mechanisms to have your belief recharged. This is where having a confidant (usually a peer) works so well – they can be a sounding board to whom doubts are aired, and who serve to reinforce purpose.

A further support measure is to ensure that the HR team is involved in the strategic purpose of the *Sell! Sell! Sell!* endeavour. They will be able to advise on ways in which the range of activities involved can be effectively embedded in the organisation – and they can provide insight into the way the organisation is responding.

Leaders' checklist

- Don't be scared of talking sales – they sustain everyone!
- Constantly remind your team that everyone affects sales.
- Meet customers in the ways your team does – by phone, in person – and see your company from the customers' perspective.

■ Create or participate in a programme of activities that reinforce the importance of sales.

■ Ensure that your team sales performance is regularly and publicly advertised and discussed.

■ Never allow conversations that suggest or endorse the idea that sales belongs to the 'sales department'.

seven

Marketing: leading the market

Marketing is not a function, a department or a specific skill set. The organisation that limits marketing to the 'marketing department' will do just that – limit its understanding of marketing, and misconceive how it is viewed as a business externally by customers and stakeholders.

Marketing is the way an organisation presents itself to the outside world in every dimension, from the smallest detail in handling a phone call to the most expensive media campaign. It is about how it communicates itself to *all* its stakeholders, not just to its customers but also to its suppliers and partners. It is also about what it says about itself to its staff, to the very members of its world most charged with delivering its success.

Marketing is the ultimate descriptor – it is about communication, but it is not simply about words. The nature of your products, the way they are designed, how successfully they are sold, delivered and the way your services work say as much about your organisation as any campaign ever will.

Successful marketing makes a promise and delivers it, and delivers it time and time again. Unsuccessful marketing makes a promise and lets the customer down.

All too often business leaders overlook how inclusive successful marketing needs to be – they forget that every employee, every action they take and every system and process say something about the organisation, its ethos, its values and its goals. All too often, organisations promise in campaigns but fail to deliver at the operational level – good intentions in a campaign not translated into actions.

As a leader, you are chief marketing officer – you must embody the external promises of the organisation, and ensure that your whole team does the same.

Marketing is everyone

'Marketing' is not a department. Everyone in an organisation is a marketeer and says something about their organisation.

Frequency – forever.
Key participants – everyone.
Leadership rating ***

Objective

How often do you feel infuriated by the service experience that does not match the fine (fancy) words of a corporate advertising campaign? By the hotel chain that promises a superior experience tailored to business needs, which turn out to be delivered by surly, ill-informed staff? By the frequent flyer service that offers the exclusivity of lounges, but in fact delivers to a singularly non-exclusive large number of travellers? By the plumbing service that offers rapid response, only to be executed by technicians too overworked to commit to an appointment time they can keep? By the call centres offering easy access to answers to all your questions that keep you on hold for periods long enough to hear their entire repertoire of recorded musical favourites?

I have to say that in the twenty-first century business world my expectations are more frequently disappointed than they are met or exceeded. The sad outcome – and I very much doubt that I am alone – is that I have learned to manage them downwards to limit frustration. But I do not think this is the outcome of a massive confidence trick on the part of businesses in general – these days there are few monopolies that impose high switching costs, and it is easy for customers – be they consumer or corporate – to switch suppliers. In fact, it has probably never been easier to do so.

*Your objective is to ensure that within your team everyone delivers what they promise in **all their interactions with customers**.*

Context

The intriguing question, then, is why is it so often the case that the customer is let down? The problem rests substantially with the overall concept of 'marketing'. Leave to one side debates whether marketing is a function (the team that does adverts and direct mail), or a strategic approach to product development and position (using some combination of Porter and BCG models). Really it is simple – marketing embraces every *engagement*, every point of contact, between an organisation and its stakeholders. It is your role as leader to ensure that your organisation understands this principle so well that it is in its corporate blood.

This is a tall order – it means that every e-mail, every letter, every phone call, every order, every package, every meeting, every greeting, *every detail of every action* must make a statement about the organisation – its beliefs, values and core proposition.

Challenge

Your role is to develop this understanding – to help your organisation to see itself in the customers' eyes; to frame its behaviour at all times from the customer's perspective; and to refine all aspects of engagement in a way that first and foremost meets the customers' needs, and not the needs of internal convenience. There is no get-out for anyone in this approach – hence *marketing is everyone*; not a department, not a product plan, but a corporate way of life.

No leader can possibly see all areas of engagement or realistically monitor them. Above all else you lead by example, and challenge all issues from a customer's perspective – you are the ultimate customer champion. You exhort beyond any level that seems natural on the basis – so critical to leadership in general – that leadership messages are rarely believed unless repeated. You also look and listen for signs that indicate the customer is not being put first, for example:

■ statements that 'we have always done things this way' –

indicating that the status quo is thoughtlessly embedded without reference to changing customer needs;

- high levels of customer complaints about repetitive issues;

- internal complaints, especially from staff dealing with customers, that issues affecting customer perceptions are repeatedly ignored despite promises of remediation;

- any statements or processes that clearly place the needs of internal bureaucracy ahead of customer requirements.

This has to be a relentless process – the effective leader can never let go, never let up on the dominance of the customer. You have to be tediously repetitive, constantly enforcing the view that everyone affects the positioning and reputation of the organisation.

Success

Your main tactic in reinforcing the dominance of the customer is to ensure that the concept of 'marketing is everyone' becomes an approach in everyone's attitude to their work.

- **First days** – from your first day talk repeatedly about the customer, their importance as the lifeblood of the organisation. Make it a way of life that issues are seen through the prism of customer experience.

- **All staff** – constantly emphasise the notion that all staff – *all staff* – have a direct or indirect bearing on customer interaction, and that all staff are key to the overall marketing proposition.

- **Marketing for all** – refuse to allow marketing to be the preserve of 'marketing' (in the same way that customer service is not the preserve of 'customer service') and idealise the notion that marketing should be on everyone's job description.

- **Marketing is everyone** – introduce the concept as a formal programme, if needs be, to encourage departmental and interdepartmental analysis of how all staff affect your core propositions.

- **Customer journey** – reinforce this marketing concept with the notion of the 'customer journey' (see *The customer journey 1: customer experience*), which is a further analytical tool to see the business through its customers' eyes.

- **Performance** – refuse to tolerate poor performance in relation to customer experience. Say so, and be seen to say so.

- **Surveys** – all these actions should be supported by regular and detailed customer experience and satisfaction surveys.

This is a case where you will have to keep on making statements that may sound odd, and you will often be met with incomprehension or downright disagreement. Many will continue to feel and think that marketing *is* for the marketing department.

The chief marketing officer will have his or her own personalised sales and marketing campaign to prove them wrong.

Leaders' measures of success

- → Sales growth.
- → Operating profit percentage.
- → Market share percentage and growth.

Pitfalls

Much success in any organisation is driven by the effective implementation of careful plans. So also the reverse – plan, but fail to attend to the detail of putting the plan into effect – and the risk of failure rises exponentially. So with *marketing is everyone*:

- **you start talking about 'marketing is everyone' but then stop** – this inconsistency and lack of commitment makes 'marketing' another management shooting star, coming and leaving without trace;

- **you refer to marketing as a department** – this silo approach allows a wide range of staff to disclaim any responsibility for marketing impact on customers;

■ **customer-facing strategies in different teams are unrelated** – in this scenario, where teams are customer-orientated but disconnected, 'marketing is everyone' becomes marketing by everyone for no one, fragmentation meaning there's no common view of the customer;

■ **you fail to respond to continual lapses in an integrated marketing approach** – commitment not supported by enforcement runs the risk of becoming no commitment at all, because words are not matched by deeds, and the 'marketing is everyone' philosophy becomes shallow;

■ **the organisation doesn't listen to feedback** – marketing is not a one-way process, it must incorporate feedback mechanisms. Any marketing commitment which is deaf to customer feedback is deluding itself about its effectiveness.

The message is *follow through* – only ruthless and determined commitment will make 'marketing is everyone' a reality.

Leaders' checklist

■ Be clear with yourself that *marketing is everyone* is a way of business life, not a slogan.

■ Link *marketing is everyone* to the concepts around *the customer journey*.

■ Talk about it, talk about it and talk about it – until you're blue in the face, and even then it's probably not enough!

■ Think of yourself as your team's chief marketing officer.

■ Try never to refer to marketing as a department.

■ Ensure that 'marketing' plans are understood and supported by all teams, not simply the one called 'marketing'.

■ Get detailed feedback about customer reactions to any part of your team's business activities, review the feedback personally and be seen to act on it.

■ Ensure that customer feedback is discussed openly in all your team meetings.

■ Be clear about the measures of success for marketing – sales, profits and market share.

Branding and organisational identity

All organisations use names for themselves or their products –
some become 'brands'. You must play a part in separating brand
from internal organisational identity.

Frequency – constant, it's existential.
Key participants – all staff whether they realise it or not.
Leadership rating ***

Objective

A *brand* can be a trademark or a name that is associated with
a specific product or service. When it becomes widely known,
it is said to have achieved *brand recognition*. For consumers the
said brand represents defined added value, and for its owner
the brand may command premium prices and have an intrinsic
tradable value, often called *brand equity*. Successful brands acquire
physical characteristics that create a so-called *brand identity*,
which may include a recognisable logo or phrase. Ultimately an
organisation becomes the guardian of its brand or brands for its
customers, and *brand management* seeks to align all the organisation's activities to underpin defined *brand values*.

A distinction can be made between contact with the brand and
the imagining of it – these are often called *brand experience* (what
it's like to use the product) and *brand image* (what we think about
the product) respectively.

In parallel, the organisation that owns and exploits product
brands makes decisions about its *corporate identity*. In some cases
(for example Apple and the BBC) its identity will match its
products and services. In some cases the organisation itself will
have a defining *business brand*, a corporate name, as which it is

a manager of a portfolio of product brands. The organisation may also state *organisational values* which are sometimes found in *ethics* or *values statements*. In this respect the CEO becomes the *corporate brand and values manager*.

Brands are an increasingly valuable asset for organisations when many products and services are becoming commoditised. It is therefore vital that at every level an organisation aligns its use of names, its activities and its values with its chosen brands – and that it understands in a *hierarchy of brands* necessary similarities and differences between who its staff work for and what they sell.

*Every leader at every level must see themselves as a brand manager – and recognise how their **actions add to or subtract from brand value**.*

Context

Working for an organisation is like playing in a sports team or joining a club – there is a sense of *belonging*. The experience of *belonging* is a very powerful tool in corralling shared team actions in favour of the customer, in contributing to the development of company brands whose reality matches their promise. This is at its most powerful when *what it feels like to belong matches what it feels like to be a customer*.

Most people want to feel that they belong to the organisation they are employed by. They want the 8–10 hours per day they dedicate to their employer to be 'worth it' on more than a monetary level. They are looking for the rewards of self-worth and pride. They also want their organisation to succeed through capturing dominant market share.

Brand can thus be a symbol of *value* to the customer and of *belonging* to the employee. It becomes a recognisable but intangible mechanism that binds customers and employees in a shared community.

Challenge

Brand and identity management can seem rarefied and even remote, especially if you don't work in a consumer goods business, traditionally the one most associated with brands. But the democratisation enabled by the internet – with far greater access to many more businesses by far more people – has created a 'flat earth'[1] where brands from all types of businesses can very much more rapidly rise (and fall). Businesses have to avoid three major risks.

- **Brand ambiguity** – where it is unclear what a brand represents and therefore difficult to align supporting activities effectively – for example the service delivery in a hotel fails to match the promise of advertising campaigns.
- **Brand casualness** – a brand is used in inconsistent ways suggesting a lack of policing in its application – for example the use of a variety of visual logos.
- **Brand confusion** – where it is unclear what the brand is *at all* – for example an organisation uses a wide range of varying brands with no apparent strategy, often mixing product and corporate names randomly.

You may not be in a position where you can directly influence the application of brands but you can:

- identify where brands are unclear in meaning;
- identify where brands are being used inconsistently or casually;
- emphasise to your own teams the importance of brand management;
- convey issues with brands to those colleagues who can influence branding.

This is a specialised area, as much influenced by psychology as by 'management'. You may find it a tough one to engage in – your

---

1 See *The World is Flat* by Thomas L. Friedman, 2nd edition (Penguin Books, 2007).

primary challenge is to be both aware of and sensitive to the issues and risks.

Success

I suggest that to engage successfully in branding and identity you follow six steps.

1 Be aware that branding and identity are issues that ultimately affect the value of the organisation, and that they can be influenced by the actions of all staff.

2 Be clear that *brand* and *organisational identity* are not necessarily the same thing.

3 Know there are at least eight types of brand (a *brand hierarchy*):

- **company name** – the name of the parent organisation, e.g. 'Corus';

- **individual brand** – the name of a specific product, e.g. 'Marmite';

- **attitude brand** – a lifestyle statement, e.g. 'Starbucks';

- **icon brand** – a statement of aspiration, e.g. 'Apple';

- **derived brand** – a component of a large product becomes a brand in its own right, e.g. 'Intel';

- **extended brand** – a brand is extended from its original product, e.g. Ferrari-branded clothes;

- **multi-brand** – a provider chooses to adopt several brands in the same category;

- **own brand** – a reseller of brands starts labelling goods with its own name, e.g. 'Tesco'.

Your organisation can use any number of them.

4 Recognise that, quite separately, your organisation may use internal, structurally descriptive nomenclature. Let's say there was a business called *Anderson* operating in hotels where the hotel brands are *Russell* (premium) and *Mark* (mid-market). This might include:

- management reporting structures ('Anderson Management Committee');
- legal entities ('Anderson India Limited');
- regional management entities ('Anderson Asia');
- country management entities ('Anderson Singapore');
- functional entities ('Anderson Catering');
- market sectors ('Anderson Premium Hotels Group');
- divisions ('Anderson Premium Hotels Group, Asia');
- business units ('Russell Hotels, China');
- product units ('Mark Hotels').

None of these is necessarily a brand.

5 Understand that ultimately 'brand management' is an all-company and not a marketing department-only activity. No one is excluded from responsibility for brand performance.

6 Believe and engage in your role in raising awareness of the issues and risks associated with brand management.

Leaders' measures of success

→ Your organisation knows what its brands are.

→ Your organisation has a process for managing brands.

→ There are clearly published value statements about your brands.

Pitfalls

The biggest risk to branding does not lie in branding itself – it lies in the nature of the host organisation, since in the end the values of brands (designed or unintentional) represent their 'parent'; and since the parent organisation can influence the financial value of brands.

These risks crystallise when, for example:

- an organisation is unclear what it stands for – it lacks a clear or convincing Vision (for example what range of services should the BBC produce?);

- an organisation's statements fail to match is brand proposition – most famously perhaps when Gerald Ratner described his jewellery chain's products as 'crap';
- an organisation's practices fail to match its image – for example allegations that Nike use child labour in manufacturing;
- a product or service fails to deliver promised characteristics – for example perceived lack of quality in the British Leyland car brands in the 1970s.

Your role is to be part of a system of brand monitoring, alert in particular to:

- a lack of clarity of brand purpose and meaning;
- a lack of consistency in and commitment to implementation.

If you do not listen and watch, day by day quite literally, to what is 'said' about and done to brands to safeguard their integrity, then you become complicit in potential brand deterioration and devaluation.

Leaders' checklist

- Be aware that labels in organisations are more than just *names* – they can become brands with independent value.
- Understand the distinction between brand and organisational identity – and that the two may be different.
- Take the time and trouble to understand brand hierarchy – learn the eight types of brand.
- Remember that brand management is not simply about design and logos – it's about what all the organisation's actions say about a product or service.
- Remember too that all staff have a potential impact on brand value.

- Regard yourself, as a leader, as a brand manager – you are the champion and the guardian of all brand values.

- Be prepared to be ruthless in enforcing brand values – they are like any values; once compromised, soon lost.

Leading product development

New product development is the lifeblood of almost all organisations. All leaders, directly or indirectly, contribute to a culture in which products can meet customers' needs.

Frequency – increasingly short cycles.
Key participants – driven by specialists, but the right attitude encourages or deters all staff.
Leadership rating **

Objective

The basis of profitable business relationships is that an organisation sells to its customers a product or products at a price and at a volume sufficient to generate a level of return on invested capital greater than that obtainable through (simpler) moneymarket investments. This depends crucially on delivering what customers want, and in turn understanding and acting on the ways in which customer requirements change.

The core objective of product development is to be ahead of today's profitable transactions, developing what will be sold tomorrow and thereafter. Very simply, then, successful product development depends on:

- understanding what it is about today's products that is popular (or not) – the *actual*;
- engaging with customers to learn what else they might want to purchase, and how the way they buy may change – the *probable*;
- tracking how technology is changing what *can* be offered to customers – the *possible*.

You role is to ensure that your organisation is product sensitive – that is, **sensitive to what customers want and to the possibilities of innovation.**

Context

How do you engender in an organisation a spirit of innovation that is not so proud and so bound to what it has already achieved that it is deaf to customer feedback, that is prepared to challenge norms and the status quo and that is restless enough to think what may seem the unthinkable?

There are no rules for innovation, by definition. Some organisations (famously 3M) enable so-called 'skunk works' by allowing staff to devote a percentage of their paid employment to their own ideas. Others attempt to formalise seed-corn investment in innovation through creating ring-fenced innovation or venture capital funds.

To foster innovation you must take an *innovative stance*. You must be:

- **countercultural** – ready to reject any suggestion that a specific approach is the organisation's 'way';
- **iconoclastic** – prepared to challenge any and all accepted norms;
- **open-minded** – receptive to any ideas, however 'left field';
- **pluralistic** – open to ideas wherever and whoever they come from;
- **cannabalistic** – unafraid of ideas that threaten existing business;
- **international** – eager to learn from many cultures;
- **generationalist** – anxious to learn from new generations with fresh perspective;
- **open to new boundaries** – unlimited in thinking;
- **humble** – aware that others have the best ideas.

In whatever role you take, if you successfully engender innovation you do so not through processes, but through creating an *innovative culture* in which ideas themselves are never penalised.

Challenge

The counterweight to ideas is *risk* – how much an organisation is prepared to wager on the new and the untried. At one level, this is about portfolio management. Whether you are running an entire business or simply an advertising campaign for a specific product, you take a measured view of the proportion of resources you are prepared to allocate to 'risk'. The essence here is an estimation of the cost of the failure of innovation and its overall impact.

And it is failure – or rather the *fear of failure* – that is the biggest challenge to innovation and product development. As leader you must emphasise – *and be heard to say* – that:

- failure is normal;
- failure is a part of progress;
- failure is key to learning;
- if you haven't failed, you haven't risked enough;
- the worst failure is not to learn from failure.

In this way you blend *innovative culture* with *supported risk-taking*.

Success

Within a culture of innovation and risk-taking, you must approach product development with a very clear set of seven principles.

- **Customer expectations** – the fundamental expectation of many customers will be for new or enhanced products delivering more for less cost. The challenge in product development is not to assume that price is always declining but to focus on delivering *value* – the right price, not the lowest price. Product development will often be informed by market surveys and detailed customer feedback, but a key element in innovation is to generate products that customers would never have imagined, and being unafraid to do so.

- **Speed of change** – all customers, consumer and corporate, are becoming ever more demanding as globalisation and technological innovation drive increasing competition. No product development approach can be viewed as sequential – i.e. one new product or service follows another. The innovative organisation is already planning the next product innovation (*and the next*) before the current 'new' innovation has even been launched!

- **Speed to market** – consequently, development processes have had to be massively accelerated and continue to be so. Elapsed times between conceiving and executing product or service innovations are continually shortening. This is putting new demands on planning processes, staff requirements, supplier strategies and relationships, and logistics. Innovation is a fundamentally uncomfortable, fast and bumpy ride!

- **Technology** – technology is not the be-all-and-end-all, but is an enabling prerequisite for innovation. It should be seen not just as *part* of new products or services, but as a key driver of process, logistical and supply changes that reduce cost and shorten development time.

- **Understanding core competence** – being nimble demands a clear insight into competence, along with knowing what your organisation does (and should do) well and what should be outsourced. This will change over time, driven less by the conventional view that outsourcing is an opportunity to reduce costs and increase efficiency, but more by the realisation that decisions on what to *insource* are crucial insights about how an organisation adds value.

- **Global skills sourcing** – the best innovation junks any notion that homegrown ideas and resources are the best. Globalisation has pluralised and dispersed knowledge and skill. Strategies for sourcing any element of the innovation development and production supply chain should seek the best available suppliers based on skill, not on where they are.

■ **Integration of post-sales service** – successful product development remembers that the customer experience has hardly begun when a sale is made. Interactions with customers post-sale are part of a 'think-through' development process which inextricably binds sales and service *from the beginning* of the development cycle.

Successfully leading innovative product development is in essence a matter of *attitude*.

Leaders' measures of success

➤ The percentage of expenditure which relates to innovation.

➤ The percentage of income which comes from products created in the last two years.

➤ The lead-time to bring new products to market.

Pitfalls

Successful product development can be undermined if you:

■ **Only listen to customers** – sometimes customers don't have the best ideas and have to be led to innovations they never imagined (for example the iPod); the successful leader avoids being a slave to customer surveys;

■ **Regularly reject new ideas** – you should encourage the out-of-the-box and never be seen to defend 'the way we do things';

■ **Blame failure** – as failure is the necessary cost of innovation, sometimes 'having a go' but failing must be celebrated as much as success;

■ **See innovation as a function** – good ideas, especially those that challenge the status quo, are the preserve of no one, and the leader must encourage innovation as a culture for all;

- **Smother innovation in bureaucracy** – the temptation to analyse new ideas excessively is very great, as a means of limiting risk; but sometimes (within an overall portfolio of risk) experimentation and trial-and-error are the best ways of testing ideas.

Perhaps the greatest challenge is posed by leaders themselves. The more senior they become, and the more they become responsible for, the more they may feel they have to lose, both professionally and personally. Promotion and career ambition may then become the enemy of innovation. The *only* response to this is to regard innovation as a badge of, not a barrier to, success.

Leaders' checklist

- Remember that product development essentially depends on creating a culture of innovation.

- Lead an innovation culture where ideas are cherished and celebrated.

- Recognise that successful innovation demands a fresh approach to all aspects of supply chain management and customer engagement.

- Be seen and heard to encourage countercultural and iconoclastic thinking.

- Know that risks have to be taken and managed within a portfolio approach.

- Be unafraid of failure and be seen and be heard to say that failure is the acceptable price for true innovation.

- Be honest in recognising that product development requires ever quicker responses to changing customer demands and ever speedier development cycles.

Internet transformations

The internet has revolutionised commerce. Its power has to be harnessed to drive business improvement across all areas of customer engagement

Frequency – requires responses at a very rapid rate.
Key participants – increasingly all staff.
Leadership rating * (soon to be ****)**

Objective

For too many 'the web' began as and remains an electronic billboard – slightly more sophisticated, but essentially static and unidirectional. There are very few – notable well-known exceptions are perhaps Amazon, Apple, Facebook and Twitter – which have really unlocked the power of the web to make it dynamic and interactive. Despite its power and ubiquity, many use Google, for example, as an accelerated 'look-up' directory, and even though YouTube has democratised the power to broadcast it remains essentially one-way.

The marketing opportunity presented by the web is to find, engage and interact with customers in wholly new ways, to change the customer's place and role in business structure and, perhaps most of all, to transform marketing mindsets so that customers are no longer seen as being on the receiving end of communications.

A paradigm shift is taking place in the use of media technology (see table opposite).

*Your objective is to recognise this paradigm shift for what it is – a **fundamental rebalancing of relationships between producers and consumers**.*

Old media	New media
■ Static	■ Dynamic
■ Broadcast	■ Interactive
■ Point-to-point	■ Mobile
■ Producer-led	■ User-generated
■ Closed target community	■ Open target community
■ Regulated	■ Liberalised
■ Producer sets terms of trade	■ Consumer sets terms
■ Producer controls communication tools	■ Consumer has same tools
■ Communication skills in 'closed shop'	■ Communication skills owned by all
■ Producer selects target market	■ Consumer opts into market

Context

The world is now divided into *digital natives* and *digital immigrants*[1]:

■ **digital native** – anyone born into the era of mobile digital media (iPods, MP3s), unlikely to be older than 21;

■ **digital immigrant** – everyone else.

Such a bold distinction – insightfully radical to some, wilfully simplistic to others – describes a major cultural, behavioural and attitudinal shift. It depicts a wholesale, generational shift in the way consumers expect to receive and transact information and entertainment. And with it comes a paradigm shift in who controls and has access to data, and who understands and uses enabling technologies.

As the number and power of digital natives grows, many organisations will be forced to respond to this generational change with teams most likely largely made up of digital immigrants. This does, or will, require organisations to undertake major

---

1 These terms were coined by Marc Prensky in *Digital Natives, Digital Immigrants* (MCB University Press, 2001).

educational programmes to learn about new technologies and new consumer behaviours.

Quite simply, you need to know who your digital immigrants and digital natives are, and to shape your response to this paradigm change by being realistic about where your overall team sits on the native–immigrant spectrum.

Challenge

The biggest single challenge you face is to get your team to confront change. You have to find ways of enabling them to face the enormity of the paradigm shift being experienced.

One approach is to present a series of change facts. For example:

- the number of years it took for TV to reach an audience of 50 million was 38 – for Facebook it was 2;
- the top ten jobs advertised in 2010 didn't exist in 2004;
- the number of Google searches per month was 31 billion in 2009 – it was 2.1 billion in 2006;
- the amount of information created in a year now reaches 4×10^{19} bytes, more than in the previous 5000 years put together;
- the number of internet devices was 1000 in 1984 – and 1 000 000 000 in 2008[2].

What these facts highlight is both the *scale* and the *rate* of change. You have to stress how the change facing your organisation is *big* and *fast*.

Success

In the face of a sea change, you must be bold enough to change the terms of debate within your team. You must adopt an interrogative style, demanding answers to a whole new set of questions.

---

2 Taken from *Shift Happens: Education 3.0*, at www.youtube.com/user/campusvue

New question	Old question
▪ Who are the competitors I haven't thought of?	▪ What are my competitors doing?
▪ What are the technologies I haven't heard of?	▪ How do I apply technology X?
▪ How do I create new products and services using internet technology?	▪ How do I apply internet technology to existing products?
▪ Who are the customers I have never thought of?	▪ What do my customers think?
▪ What information about me does my customer have?	▪ What information shall I let my customer have?
▪ How would a 17-year-old digital native tackle this issue?	▪ What does my experienced team think?
▪ What industry am I in?	▪ What is the industry consensus about change?
▪ How do I reshape my business from scratch?	▪ How do I make incremental changes?
▪ What is my new business model?	▪ How does the internet affect my business model?
▪ What fundamental changes will take place in the next six months?	▪ What changes do we expect in the next three years?

As with any paradigm shift, your role is to embrace it, not hope it will go away – to become an active insider and not remain a passive outsider. No leader can expect to have the answers to all the questions, but you can make sure the questioning happens.

Leaders' measures of success

➤ Your business talks about digital natives and digital immigrants.

➤ Your business measures innovation. How?

➤ The proportion of sales transactions that are digital.

Pitfalls

The risk lies in the leaders who think changes don't affect them, their teams or their organisations. Those who stand in the face of such a shift may find themselves outflanked. Consider for example:

- Which music providers adopted file-sharing as an opportunity rather than a threat when it emerged?
- Which 24-hour news organisations planned for speedier news delivery to be available via Twitter?

These two examples are real lessons about change defeating complacency. Today you must be prepared to confront the uncomfortable and sometimes downright scary. Telltale signs of resistance are:

- **the leader who defends the status quo on the basis of tradition** – tradition is, I am afraid, the refuge of the complacent;
- **the leader who doesn't use social media** – how can you understand the way digital natives live?
- **the leader who sees new media as a continuation of producer-led, control-based communication** – failure to understand the power of 'user generated' communication betrays a lack of insight into the changed balance of power.

Many leaders can't be digital natives – but they can admit their existence and ensure that their insights are valued.

Leaders' checklist

- Recognise that the digital era represents a *paradigm shift* – everything is up for grabs.

- Understand the profound difference between *digital natives* and *digital immigrants*.

- Help your team to realise that if they are over 21 they are likely to be digital immigrants and that they need to learn from the perspective of digital natives.

■ Accept that you will need to lead a process of tough interrogation of received assumptions.

■ Appreciate that today's scale and rate of change are unprecedented, and that the nature of change itself is changing.

■ Consider – given the scale of change – identifying digital champions in your team.

■ Remember that many insights into the nature of change will come from organisations you do not recognise as competitors or partners.

eight

Suppliers and partners: leading together

All organisations consume a range of goods and services on which they depend, very often critically, for the successful, efficient and timely delivery of their own products and services. Quite normally their reputation depends on their suppliers' performance; quite normally also, their own customers have no idea who their suppliers are, and on whom they actually also depend.

The management of suppliers has spawned a range of disciplines and/or approaches over the last three decades, for example:

- **supply chain management** – the management of a network of related businesses involved in the ultimate provision of products and services required by end-user customers;

- **procurement** – the acquisition of goods and/or services at the best possible total cost of ownership, in the right quality and quantity, at the right time, in the right place and from the right source;

- **total quality management** – a management strategy to embed awareness of quality in all organisational processes;

- **Six Sigma** – a system (developed by Motorola) for improving the quality of process outputs by identifying and removing the causes of defects (errors) and variability in manufacturing and business processes.

In essence, the entire process of 'purchasing' has been hugely systematised and professionalised. But what none of these approaches really conveys is *what are suppliers for?*

This part of the book demonstrates that to be an effective leader you must reach out to suppliers and see them as part of your organisation's leadership team, engage with them as equals rather than subordinates and regard suppliers not as organisations with whom you spend cash, but as partners on your pathway to success.

Building relationships

Partner relationships are a vital part of a leader's armoury. Much depends on the informal success of interpersonal relationships rather than formal structures.

Frequency – constant.
Key participants – all staff, knowingly or unknowingly.
Leadership rating ****

Objective

When you manage a business or a team, you can draw a hierarchy depicting the organisational structure in which you work – who you work for, who works for you. You can undertake a SWOT analysis that places your organisation within a competitive framework populated by key industry players. You could go further and undertake a Porterian analysis of the broader competitive forces shaping your industry, with additional insights into potential or new entrants and the supply chain. You can identify all the partners with whom you have contracts and you can use sophisticated customer relationship management (CRM) models to drill ever deeper into customer buying habits and patterns.

This is, if you like, what is formal and overt – the tangible data that depicts the network of trading, contractual and competing relationships, which define the commercial patterns, successes and failures of your organisation. It is in no sense superficial because it will inform your Vision, your strategy and your tactics, and dominate the daily cut-and-thrust of work. But – and this is a very substantial *but* – of equal and possibly greater significance is the network of relationships that *don't* appear in any organisational chart, strategic analysis or list of contracts, but which may be the most powerful relationships of all.

*You learn how to identify such relationships, which ones to develop and which to avoid, and what the very specific skills are that you require to **navigate such essentially unchartered territory**.*

Context

You must have the *nous* to see where key non-formal relationships are around you. These relationships might be between:

- your peers;
- colleagues who work for you;
- peers or colleagues and major competitors;
- peers or colleagues and major suppliers;
- peers or colleagues and significant industry partners/trade associations.

There will be no environment in which such relationships are absent, and no environment where they may not act as a significant brake on your plans (and even career prospects). This presents the most challenging of balancing acts. Clearly you cannot live your leadership life second-guessing what other people may think, or allowing assumptions about the unseen influence of others to cloud your judgement – the ultimate effect of being seen to do so undermining your reputation for integrity and credibility. But equally you will know that the leverage of these non-formal relationships against you is enormous and potentially frustrating.

Challenge

It is vital that you do not allow yourself to be sucked into history, and allow that history (which will determine the relationships you encounter, and their tenor) to drive your approach and behaviour. You must at all times remain in your own stance with your independence and your value set. The drag effect of the status quo will be at its most powerful in this regard.

Relationship building is a currency that can be golden. You will find that the power of the reputation you achieve in building relationships can have a dramatic multiplier effect:

- as people learn of your approach they will be more ready to see you;

- as they learn to trust you they will open up more, create deeper relationships with you and provide you with deeper access into their own networks.

Be clear with yourself and your team – relationships are not an optional extra. Managing them effectively is at the heart of effective performance.

Success

You must have a relationship strategy – this has six elements.

- **Your team** – within your team, ensure that the importance of the full range of known and potentially unknown relationships is understood. Make sure that your team understands that managing such relationships is a real source of potential added value.

- **Network mapping** – construct a 'map' of the key known relationships that affect your team, inside and outside the business. The more complex this is, the more essential is the need to draw or write this down. Understand as best you can the current tenor of these relationships – what the history is, whether they are broadly positive or negative, what the potential effect of the relationships is on your team and business performance.

- **Network programme** – design a programme for managing the known relationships within a priority ranking. Communicate with and arrange to meet key stakeholders in these relationships. Make this programme a key priority in the allocation of your time, and recognise that this is an ongoing and not a one-off process.

- **Relationship assessments** – assess the state of 'known' relationships. Dispassionately reassess their value and identify which require development or reconstructive attention. Re-evaluate the priority attached to all of them.

- **Discover the unknown** – use the process of engaging in the 'known' relationship network as a voyage of discovery. Work the relationships you know about to begin to construct the map and pattern of currently 'unknown' relationships.

- **Relationship management** – be seen to manage relationships in a certain way. Make it evident that you value relationships and have a consistent and professional approach to them. Demonstrate this approach not simply in how you talk about them but how you engage with individuals and organisations.

Success happens when you take relationships seriously, showing that they matter and investing time in building them.

Leaders' measures of success

→ You know and you tabulate all key relationships.

→ You know who manages key external stakeholder relationships in your team.

→ You have a clear set of external stakeholder relationships that you manage. You are meeting these key partners at least three times a year.

Pitfalls

Relationships matter most when you don't take them seriously. The colleagues and partners who are affected by your casualness will doubt your commitment to them and to the organisation's goals. Telltale signs that you are not taking the subject of relationships seriously are:

- **silence** – if you don't talk about them, they won't appear to matter! This is not an area for discreet working;

- **lack of respect** – if you cut across existing relationships simply because you're the boss, and don't show enough respect for them, then you will be indicating that your ego matters more than the relationships themselves;
- **lack of planning** – relationship-building needs time and thought, rushing into relationships without due regard for context is risky;
- **lack of time** – if you don't give relationship-building the time and priority it deserves, the outcome will be poor, weak and incomplete relationships and a lack of respect for you as a leader.

Failure emerges when you take don't relationships seriously, don't show they matter and don't invest time in building them.

Leaders' checklist

- Make no assumptions about relationships when you join a team – assume they are all around you, seen and unseen.

- Make no assumptions about the quality of relationships you inherit or uncover – they are usually like icebergs, with most elements hidden.

- Remember that relationship-building is for ever.

- Assess your team on their ability to identify and manage key relationships – be intolerant of sub-standard performance in this area.

- Lead from the front – be seen to be in the thick of relationships and herald the achievements that evolve.

Supplier strategies

Supplier strategies are about seeing the 'total cost' of operating your business or business unit – and managing suppliers to deliver transformational change in cost and process.

Frequency – never-ending.
Key participants – supplier partner organisations.
Leadership rating ****

Objective

The value of suppliers to a business can often be underestimated, and it is part of your role as a leader to understand the transformational impact they can have. It is too easy – and it is lazy – to see suppliers as organisations with whom you 'spend' and to regard your relationship with them as one driven by agreeing prices and managing a contract.

Expenditure within business is usually allocated to separate categories for accounting purposes – normally 'cost of sale', 'overheads' and 'capital expenditure'. It is better to see this as a *total cash cost* and to think of your expenditure in categories – for example, all expenditure on information technology or logistics, irrespective of how it is classified by accountants.

The wrong question to ask is:

- How do I reduce the cost of what I am doing?

This implies that all current activities and processes are the right ones, and that the issue is the cost of their delivery. This is an approach which might be better described as *purchasing*.

The right questions to ask include:

- What processes should I be undertaking?
- Can the processes be simplified?

▓ Who should undertake the processes?

This is *supply chain management*. You must have a completely clear view of what you want to achieve – what the deliverables or outcomes are and at what price (these are your definitions of value). You then work with suppliers in partnership on a flexible basis where you are open to any options to deliver value. This is a process that is:

▓ **challenging** – you put all assumptions to one side;

▓ **continuous** – it never stops, there is always opportunity for further change.

Perhaps the key objective is to realise that suppliers are partner change-agents – their external perspective enables a 'friendly-critical' approach in **the necessary transformations your organisation will undergo***.*

Context

Organisations often ask themselves what their *core competencies* are. Supply chain management will often provoke the consideration of *outsourcing* – i.e. what can be undertaken by third-party organisations. These two issues can be confused:

▓ **core competencies** – these are activities which add value to the customer proposition;

▓ **insourcing or outsourcing** – relates to *who* undertakes tasks and activities.

This is an important distinction because the assumption can be made that a core competence is necessarily insourced – it is not. Frequently the nature of the competence is misunderstood. Take three examples.

▓ **The luxury hotel chain** – focusing on the delivery of a premium experience does not mean that it manufactures premium linen; it knows where to buy the linen from.

▓ **The publisher famous for its book designs** – focusing on design doesn't mean that they employ the designers; it has a strong visual brand and it knows how to hire designers to deliver to its guidelines.

■ **The business school renowned for its high-quality lectures** – focusing on quality content and presentation doesn't mean that it employs the lecturers; it understands what lecture quality is and knows who the best lecturers are.

By taking a flexible and outcomes-defined approach to core competence, you will evaluate supplier partnership opportunities without predefining 'who does what'.

Challenge

The core challenge you will face is ensuring that within your team or organisation there is a clear understanding about the difference between supplier management, supply chain management, purchase ordering and procurement.

■ **Supplier management** – this is essentially relationship management between vendor and customer and is likely to focus on dealing with long-term strategies and short-term issue resolution.

■ **Supply chain management** – primarily the logistical organisation and integration of all suppliers with a primary focus on inventory and working capital management.

■ **Purchase ordering** – this is the administrative process of placing orders.

■ **Procurement** – this is the strategic approach to vendor management, reviewing process and cost reduction on a constant basis.

Procurement is a professional discipline and is the strategic foundation stone for any effective supplier programme. You must raise its profile and ensure that it is understood that procurement should very often be separated from the functional discipline to which it applies – e.g. IT specialists should not be responsible for IT procurement!

Success

The details of effective supplier management are complex, but they are based on a series of necessary attitudes which, in your role as leader, you need to inculcate within your team.

- **Partnership** – view the way you work with suppliers as a series of constructive partnerships and not adversarial stand-offs, since both parties gain most from mutual success.

- **Relationship** – getting the best from your suppliers depends on developing a relationship of trust whereby you progressively learn so much about your respective organisations that they become extensions of each other.

- **Procurement** – you must see your relationships with suppliers in terms of procurement (as described above); this is first and foremost a strategic perspective.

- **Frequency** – you must meet your strategic procurement partners on a regular face-to-face basis because this is the only way to develop the mutual trust on which success will be based.

- **Strategy and tactics** – while these are essentially strategic relationships, you must be prepared to learn, understand, manage and respond to tactical detail. Respect in your supplier relationships will grow if you are seen to get your hands dirty with detail.

- **Networks** – your business will very likely depend on a number of interconnected suppliers. You must view them as a network or community to be cultivated as a group, sharing expertise and learning.

- **Key Performance Indicators (KPIs)** – your supplier relationships must be grounded in measurable performance targets, though you should not be slave to them; they are a guide and not an objective in their own right.

- **Shared success** – no relationship will be successful unless both parties see it as a success, so your objective should always be to create 'win–win' outcomes.

- **Contracts** – all supplier relationships must be grounded in contractual/legal terms and expectations, but the day you start quoting the contract at each other is the day the relationship starts breaking down.

- **Process** – you must plan to engage suppliers in all your (relevant) processes with complete transparency. Only then can they fully engage in improvement analysis.

- **Responsibility** – similarly, you should have no preconceptions about 'who does what'. Good suppliers will always challenge the status quo and propose alternative approaches.

- **Capability** – in a world in which technology is driving massive change, you should also make no assumptions about capability. Areas in which your organisation once specialised may become rapidly overtaken by more up-to-date specialisms outside your organisation.

- **Feedback** – be as prepared to receive feedback from suppliers as you are to give it.

- **Learning** – above all else, see supplier–partner relationships as a way to learn. Your organisation cannot and will not know all it could and should.

Real success in managing suppliers comes not from programmes of innovation or cost-reduction (though these are necessary outcomes), but from your attitude towards the opportunity they represent.

Leaders' measures of success

→ You know how many suppliers you have.

→ You have quarterly reviews with all suppliers.

→ Each supplier has measurable KPIs.

Pitfalls

Because procurement is a skill set in its own right, it brings with it a specific strategic approach to thinking about the role of suppliers with any given organisation. If you don't have this specific kind of strategic thinking, the primary risk is that suppliers are seen to be *transactional* – no more than one element of a number of moving parts in your supply process. With this can come some superficial supplier management attitudes.

- **The number** – you focus on how many suppliers you have. While this is certainly one index of efficiency, there is no absolute correct number and it can be a diversion from thinking about what you want suppliers to achieve.

- **The selection** – is based primarily on cost comparisons. While this will always represent a major factor, there is a real risk that excessive focus on cost distracts from a substantial analysis of capability.

- **The management** – is founded on remote KPI analysis rather than direct supplier engagement. While KPIs are important, they don't replace active face-to-face engagement on strategy and issues.

- **The blame game** – when things go wrong (they will!) you resort to blaming suppliers (it's so easy) without necessarily thinking through all the process issues that may be at fault and to which your organisation may contribute.

Leaders' checklist

- First and foremost see suppliers as partners not adversaries – they represent a major opportunity to extend your organisation's talent pool.

- Ensure that your team understands the differences between purchasing, supply chain management, supplier management and procurement.

- Remember that knowledge about a subject doesn't make you a specialist in negotiating terms to buy it!

- Focus less on the number of suppliers you have and more on the quality and innovation they bring to your organisation.

- Be transparent about the issues and challenges in your team or organisation – openness is necessary to get the best out of suppliers.

- Encourage and enjoy a culture of mutual feedback – you and your suppliers have much to learn from each other.

Managing costs

It is easy to think about managing costs as 'cutting'. It isn't – it's about your attitude to resources and priorities; less about what you spend money on than how you think about the way you spend it.

Frequency – continuous; there is always money to be saved!
Key participants – anyone with a budget.
Leadership rating ***

Objective

As a business leader, you will inevitably have some financial responsibility. You will be expected to demonstrate financial management – in particular the ability to deliver your team's planned performance within *budget*. You must aim to apply six principles.

- **Planning** – you must be clear about your strategic and operational priorities for expenditure.
- **Contingency** – your financial planning should include provision for the unexpected.
- **Support** – you will need (unless you are an accountant) strong financial support in thinking through planning and ongoing financial issues.
- **Authority** – you must have and work within a clear structure (sometimes referred to as 'delegation of authority') regarding who is allowed to commit to what expenditure to what levels.
- **Reporting** – financial reporting should be thorough, regular and transparent so that you understand ongoing performance exactly.
- **Action** – you must use financial information to take corrective action to deliver planned performance.

*Your objective is to regard the management of cost as **a key tool for delivering performance** in a planned and systematic manner.*

Context

To manage cost effectively, you certainly don't need to be an accountant! However, it will help if you have a rudimentary understanding of the three key dynamics of financial accounting.

1   **The three pillars of your organisation's accounts:**
   - *profit and loss* – the periodic reporting of your sales and costs, and whether you are generating a profit or loss;
   - *balance sheet* – the statement of your assets (what you own) and liabilities (what you owe);
   - *cash flow* – the simple measure of whether more money comes in or goes out.

2   **The three types of costs you may be responsible for:**
   - *cost of sales* (goods sold) – those costs directly attributable (often on a unit basis) to what you sell;
   - *overheads* (expenses) – those costs related to running your operation that don't vary directly with sales;
   - *capital expenditure* – investment in a product, service or physical item with an ongoing (resaleable) value.

3   **The importance of cash** – the lesson from small and start-up businesses, namely that in the end businesses survive or fail through their ability to maintain operations by having adequate cash in the bank.

The significance of this basic understanding is not to enable you to match the ability of your accountants (you won't, and you shouldn't try), but to understand the impact of your decision-making on financial performance.

Challenge

In my experience, an organisation's ability to manage costs is largely constrained by two factors.

- **Fear** – changing planned spending usually means confronting someone else's budget, and this can be both political (you may be seen to be making a choice) and sensitive (no one likes to lose out, especially where cherished pet projects are at stake). Reducing costs may challenge strategic objectives, challenge levels of employment, challenge the organisation structure and challenge existing relationships with internal and external suppliers.

- **Inflexibility** – businesses tend to assume, over time, accepted ways of working, and cultural standards that may not be verbalised. This is what I have described elsewhere as the 'we have always done things this way' mentality. Planning to reduce costs may challenge deeply held norms. The challenge to culture becomes at least as significant as the challenge to cost.

Your role as a leader is to be brave and flexible – to deny the status quo any assumed legitimacy, to be prepared to ask uncomfortable questions, to challenge legacy assumptions and, if anything, to champion the countercultural.

Success

Finance and accounting can be complex and technical. Your success in this area will depend on you taking a fundamentally *practical* approach, in which you are seen to demonstrate not only the importance of cost management but your personal involvement in it.

- **Financial planning** – you must be deeply involved in all the financial planning of your business unit (especially at each strategy, budget and quarterly review phase), and be familiar with all the key financial drivers. You cannot leave finance to financial staff.

- **Finance relationship** – your relationship with finance staff (your finance director if you have one) is critical because you will depend on their astuteness and insight. This is one relationship you must work on intensively – you need complete confidence in the reliability of this colleague.

- **Materiality** – you must be familiar enough with the costs for which you are responsible to know what is material (i.e. to know which elements *make a difference*).

- **Contingency planning** – never plan your business area without a view of what to do if things go unexpectedly; always know in advance the corrective actions you might need to take.

- **Prioritisation** – have a clear idea of what matters and what your priorities are so that, bluntly, you know what you are prepared to sacrifice.

- **Control and delegation** – have a system of controls in place so that everyone who works for you knows what they can and can't commit to; and which ensures that you are involved in all the financial decisions you need to be.

- **Reporting** – have detailed cost reporting (at least on a monthly basis) at the level of detail *you* require, and one which passes a materiality test (i.e. you track cost at the level required for effective decision-making).

- **Public reporting** – ensure that financial reporting is transparent among your immediate colleagues so that there is a clear understanding of shared responsibility and accountability.

- **Procurement** – use the skills and techniques of procurement professionals to analyse and reduce cost systematically where the scale of cost merits it.

- **Outsourcing and insourcing** – have an open mind about the merits of insourcing; sometimes the continuous use of external resources can be more expensive than dedicated internal resources. Don't set outsourcing up as a cost-saving inevitability.

■ **Next-stage reductions** – as you task your team to think about opportunities to reduce cost, begin to think about the stage after next; the next areas for examination that your colleagues are unaware of.

■ **Process reviews** – encourage all your staff to analyse their business functions as a series of processes to identify process improvements that are capable of delivering economies.

■ **Activity reviews** – further challenge your staff to identify activities that can be eliminated completely.

■ **Technology reviews** – identify all manual tasks and seek where it is plausible to replace them with cheaper automated alternatives.

■ **Evolutionary thinking** – stand back from all the activity described above and think about how your business area is evolving. Consider structural changes that could further drive down costs.

The length and depth of this series of actions itself indicates the complexity of managing cost. It requires a wide range of financial and personal skills, an acute sensitivity to the cultural impact of cost management, a simultaneously panoramic and detailed view of your business area, and an ability to analyse the immediate, the medium- and the long-term.

Leaders' measures of success

→ You have benchmarked your costs as a percentage of sales with your industry peers.

→ Your costs as a percentage of sales are on an annual downward trend.

→ You have undertaken process, activity and technology reviews.

Pitfalls

The main risk in financial and cost management leadership is to fail to give yourself room to manoeuvre, especially if you:

- plan with no contingency;
- make too many commitments and leave the 'cupboard bare';
- have too loose control over what is spent;
- have poor financial reporting and transparency about expenditure;
- can't think flexibly about different ways to act.

So the moral as far as cost management is concerned is to expect the unexpected and plan for it!

Leaders' checklist

- Make a point of learning the 'pillars' of finance in an operational business – profit and loss, balance sheet and cash flow.

- Understand the three types of cost you may be responsible for, and how they affect the business differently.

- Never forget that 'cash is king'.

- Don't be afraid to take on the fear and to tackle the inertia which may inhibit an honest appraisal of opportunities to reduce costs.

- Be aware of how complex the management of cost is – how multi-dimensional it is.

- Prioritise a good relationship with your finance 'person' – this is worth its weight in gold.

- Remember at all times the mantra of procurement professionals – businesses can *always* save 5–10 per cent.

part

nine

Learning: leadership development

When I was 27, I was privileged to undertake a company-sponsored full-time MBA. My then boss thought it was a complete and utter waste of time, likely to be a year spent indulged in discussing 'managementspeak' with little or no practical benefit. His view was that good management (I don't think he would have distinguished this from leadership) comes naturally, and that in essence you should 'get on with it'.

He said this as the most brilliant natural leader I have ever met – he did indeed just get on with it, but the rarity of seeing someone with natural leadership skills only goes to emphasise how unusual it is.

I do not subscribe to the view that great leaders are born with leadership skills, and that they somehow belong to an exclusive group closed to any aspirants. Yes it is true that, for some, leadership of the kind I am describing in this book does come naturally and they are blessed with the instinctive skills needed to get the most out of their colleagues. But these leaders are few and far between, and they are the lucky ones. For the rest of us leadership is a matter of experience and confidence – increasing our deftness as we learn what works and what doesn't, as we become honed to the sometimes very challenging role of leading teams of individuals.

But improving leadership is not only a matter of time. It is also about some specific strategies which reflect the importance both of general leadership skills and the specific knowledge you will need to lead a business in your industry. The two go together – leadership skills *are* transferable, but they are always more credible and effective when tied with insights into the world in which you work.

As a leader, you need to ensure that you create a culture of learning, a culture which demonstrates that you as an individual are always prepared to learn – and in which you create an environment where your colleagues' knowledge is respected and their opportunities to learn and grow are supported and nurtured.

The knowledge premium

Knowledge is increasingly the key – and, in some cases, the only – significant differentiator an organisation has. Your role is to celebrate and champion the acquisition, sharing and defence of knowledge.

Frequency – accelerating.
Key participants – all staff.
Leadership rating ****

Objective

As leaders we work in a business world which is increasingly commoditised. The emergence of increasingly sophisticated, but low-cost, manufacturing locations (especially in Asia) means that many goods can be sourced worldwide at competitive costs. In the same way, the emergence of large numbers of well-educated but lower-paid professional staff has driven the growth of lower-cost service centres, for example call centre, finance and legal back-office capabilities in India. And this is a process which will continue as new low-cost centres emerge to replace existing ones. So as these shifts take place, all organisations have to identify exactly where they contribute added value, and in many cases this can be defined as *knowledge*:

- of highly-specialised non-commoditisable processes, especially in engineering – e.g. in aircraft and high-speed train manufacture;

- of highly specialised information-rich service processes;

- of technology and how it is changing business comprehensively across all aspects of product/service creation and customer interaction;

- of customers and of their behaviours – e.g. in the mobile world;

- of customer environments and cultures – e.g. HSBC as the 'world's local bank';
- of running businesses smartly in such a fast-changing and internationalised environment.

This can sound remote, perhaps, from the daily grind of running teams and businesses, but it is not. I call knowledge a 'premium' precisely because it is that – it's what will make you succeed above and beyond your competitors.

Your objective as leader is to ensure that your team knows that knowledge is key. **They need to know what they need to know**.

Context

Knowledge is a key factor in managing change. Knowing that you need to learn, and that you need to learn increasingly fast, is a clear indicator of the demands, rapidity and complexity of change. And that change will manifest itself in a wide variety of ways, some predictable but many not:

- the accelerating capacity of computing processes;
- the rapid emergence of new industry capabilities in so-called emerging markets;
- the huge growth in emerging-market middle classes, notably in India and China;
- significant growth in the availability of complex data 'on the move';
- the convergence of traditional computing, telecommunications and media worlds to enable and empower new market entrants capable of delivering paradigm changes.

This is to name but five key shifts, any one of which can – and probably is – radically changing the competitive landscape of your business. To be able to meet the scale of this change requires you to recognise it for what it is – *a new industrial revolution*.

Challenge

The flipside of change is the challenge of time. The most significant business challenge you face right now is not simply recognising the nature of many major shifts taking place, but in appreciating the *scale* and *pace* of change. This requires you to challenge what may be some core and institutionalised assumptions within your industry, marketplace and organisation.

■ Who do you regard as competitors? And how often do you ask this question?

■ Who *are* your customers? And what do you know about your potential customers? How often do you investigate this?

■ How and how often do you measure what customers think of you?

■ How long does it take you to get a new product or service to market?

■ Do your investment models adequately reflect current forecasts of product and service life cycles?

■ How often do you change your organisation structures to meet the demands of the business environment?

It is tough, but you have to play your role in creating and sustaining a culture that is never satisfied with where it is, that is restless about the change it faces and the changes it needs to make in and of itself, and that is constantly challenging the status quo.

The driver to achieve this is knowledge – a relentless upskilling in understanding the business environment and your capability to respond to it, and placing the highest level of value in the knowledge that your team possesses individually and collectively.

Success

Some organisations now have a chief knowledge officer. For your specific organisation, business unit or team this is the mantle you should adopt – the relentless champion of knowing, always underpinned by the humble acceptance that your team will know more than you in specialist areas. Setting considerable store on knowledge, showing that it matters, requires attention to several areas.

- **Leadership** – you talk about knowledge and its importance.

- **A learning culture** – across all domains of your business area you openly encourage team members to learn from experience (and yes, mistakes) and never to accept the 'rightness' of the status quo.

- **Sharing learning** – many organisations that are multi-business unit or multi-divisional have similar operational functions where people are also learning. Encourage your staff to network with them to make the most of the teachers on their doorstep.

- **Bringing learning in** – encourage your staff to be open with their suppliers about the need to learn, and create forums where experiences can be shared so that the learning network is extended outside your immediate employer.

- **Personal development linked to learning** – make sure that for your business as a whole, and for the individuals in it, you identify (at least annually) key areas where each team member needs to learn. Then support the personal development and training initiatives to support it.

- **Celebrations of success and admissions of failure** – within your organisation, and publicly so, herald success and be transparent about failure so there is never embarrassment about talking through either, and learn in equal measure from both.

- **Pushing the boundaries** – in your personal interactions with staff, try to push them to where they might be hesitant to go in learning new skills and trying out new ideas. Sometimes people need a push to follow their instincts and feel the need for support in being brave.

- **Humility and respect** – above all else, knowledge needs humility and respect to flourish. And bring humility in knowing that you don't have many of the answers, and gain the respect that comes with recognising that others do.

Creating a knowledge culture is hard – it requires a constant rejection of the present for the unknown future and is at once, therefore, exciting and unsettling.

Leaders' measures of success

→ You reduce product lead times.

→ You increase your rate of investment.

→ What is your market share? In the end this is the best measure of learning to survive and thrive.

Pitfalls

The worst position an organisation can reach is to have a *knowledge deficit* – where it is significantly lacking the insight it needs to develop in its chosen market. This can arise because:

- **learning is neglected** – there is no open admission or acceptance that learning needs to occur;
- **learning is equated with risk** – this happens when the 'new' (the 'learned') is seen as being risky through its very 'newness', and the need to learn is confused with decisions that need to be made about the learning, so the learning is suspended;
- **learning is compartmentalised** – learning takes place but is 'silo'd' and becomes devalued or lost through isolation;
- **learning is slow** – learning does take place but it is simply too slow for the pace of the marketplace it relates to, and so remains (relatively) negative in its impact;
- **learning is not respected** – the organisation does not herald the power of learning and therefore devalues its relevance and currency.

All this risks creating an 'unlearning' organisation which actually learns less about its marketplace as time goes on, loses market share and ultimately its existence.

Leaders' checklist

- Think of yourself as the chief knowledge officer.

- Be aware that much of what a business thinks it knows about its world and marketplace is already out-of-date.

- Be further aware, therefore, that most of what you need to know is currently unknown.

- Remember that knowledge is not hierarchical – you need all your team to be experts in their field.

- Never forget that knowledge respects no boundaries – it is there for the taking, especially by new competitors.

- Display humility about what you don't know and respect for others about what they do.

Awaydays

'Awaydays' are short periods of time – usually no more than one or two days – when you take your immediate colleagues to a location away from the office for an informal process of bonding and reflection.

Frequency – irregular, by definition.
Key participants – your direct reports only.
Leadership rating *

Objective

Most of us work in an employment location. Even if we work in an increasingly flexible structure that encourages home-working, the office base is the single location we have in common with our colleagues and the one which essentially defines our relationships. It is the place where we most often meet, which has formal and informal rules of behaviour and which sets the tone – itself affected by many factors (location, structure, layout, catering, recreation facilities and so on).

Work locations are necessarily *artificial* – they bring together people who wouldn't otherwise meet or socialise. They are also necessarily *transactional* – we tend to focus on getting the job done and having conversations about work. Pleasantries about our outside ('real') lives are inevitably fragmented, partial and discreet.

Work locations thus become limiting – they limit our opportunity to understand our colleagues, and what makes them tick, and to share the knowledge and experience they have that may not be highlighted by the transactional nature of shared work.

Occasional 'awaydays' – taking your team out of the office context into a less structured, less formal and more social environment – can help to break down the barriers that workplaces can erect.

*The objective of awaydays is not to create a false bonhomie, but to engender an improved team spirit through **deeper personal relationships**.*

Context

If you accept that workplaces are artificial and can create barriers, you need to understand the greater risk they also present – one of *dysfunction*. We have probably all seen circumstances where colleagues 'don't get on' and where managing the interface between them requires at best diplomacy and at worst sidestepping 'hot spots'. Such tension can have many causes, including:

- resentment of others' roles or promotion;
- frustrated ambition;
- a feeling that personal skills are overlooked or underestimated;
- misunderstandings over issues;
- a lack of clarity of roles;
- poor interpersonal skills – compounded by a lack of feedback.

This is part of business life. Awaydays can help in providing a more social setting where some of the inhibitions affecting the workplace can be removed (there is more time to talk about personal lives), and where even the sources of conflict can be confronted.

Challenge

The greatest challenge to successful awaydays is the *sceptic* – the colleague who doesn't believe in what they perceive as management sophistry – putting staff in an even more artificial setting to create essentially false goodwill. This sceptic will suggest directly or indirectly that awaydays are:

- a waste of time (and money);

- at best a distraction from daily transactional tasks;
- at worst an attempt to create a sense of teamwork that is an illusion and representative of 'managementspeak'.

I have to say quite openly that it is absolutely true that awaydays are a management collusion – in this case between good leadership and HR, and designedly so. And the only responses to scepticism are:

- **persistence** – continuing to undertake awaydays in the face of disbelief;
- **explanation** – being unembarrassed when explaining why you are doing awaydays;
- **leading by example** – persuading colleagues of the value of awaydays through their outcome.

There will always be those who doubt the value of awaydays. As leader you must confront them and show them they are wrong.

Success

The success of awaydays essentially rests in achieving a subtle balance between careful planning and unstructured informality, within a framework where your team know that you take them seriously.

- **Clarity of purpose** – as leader you make it clear very early on that you will be having awaydays, and having them regularly.
- **Frequency** – plan to have them at least once a year, preferably every six months, so that they are seen as part of a process and not as a one-off.
- **Location** – select somewhere away from the office and in an environment that is conducive to constructive thinking. Business schools, for example, are better in this regard than hotel meeting rooms.
- **Time** – allow at least one and a half days so that there is no feeling that you are in a rush between whatever came before and what comes after. A lack of time, and a pressured

agenda, introduces a stress inconsistent with an awayday's goals.

- **Agenda and objectives** – set an agenda in advance, so that the objectives of an awayday are clear, but be prepared to flex the agenda and change the contents, depending on the outcome of conversations.

- **Facilitation** – consider whether your awayday meeting would benefit from any outside facilitation. Generally outsiders disrupt team dynamics but you may decide this is exactly what you want because you take the view that your team is rather too dysfunctional or too satisfied with itself.

- **Interruption** – do not allow interruptions. Ask for phones and Blackberries to be turned off, laptops to be closed and any other planned, conflicting meetings to be rescheduled (including teleconferences).

- **Meals** – make sure there is at least one planned evening team meal – this can be an excellent way of breaking down barriers (especially through careful use of planned seating).

- **Outsiders** –include outsiders (i.e. non-direct reports) very sparingly, maybe as guest speakers for particular sessions.

- **Outcomes** – ensure that agreed outcomes are noted, actioned and reviewed.

Managing awaydays – easy as they are to organise – requires extreme deftness on your part. They are not – and cannot be run as – another set of meetings in the management calendar. Nor are they freebies designed to make staff feel good in probably more luxurious circumstances than usual. They are there for a real purpose – you must take the opportunity they present!

Leaders' measures of success

→ You hold awaydays.

→ How often are your awaydays and where are they held?

→ Your HR team believe that your awaydays are contributing to tackling issues.

Pitfalls

Probably the biggest mistake you can make is to organise awaydays but not to take them seriously for what they are – in other words, to pay lip-service to the concept allowing them to become either ordinary meetings or 'jollies' (there is a place for the 'jolly' but it is a quite different event).

Don't start awaydays if you don't intend to continue them – a start–stop approach devalues their significance and will make you look like a leader who has adopted the concept of awaydays as a fad but has then reverted to a more traditional type.

Equally, if awaydays do have the potential significance I have argued, then they may throw up major challenges to the direction of your team, the way it is run (by you) and its composition. An awayday may force you or your team to confront issues more openly, but it will not necessarily resolve them. Follow-up is vital – failure to follow-up may be more debilitating and undermining than a failure to confront issues in the first place.

Leaders' checklist

- Talk about awaydays early on in your tenure as leader – make them seem normal, and make it clear you are committed to them.

- If you hold awaydays, make sure they are regular and are seen as part of your team's processes.

- Give them a name – they acquire a life of their own and this helps to enforce their importance and difference.

- See the cost of awaydays as a minimal and highly justifiable investment in your team, and probably offering a higher return than more conventional management development.

■ Don't underestimate the importance of the venue in contributing to the success of your awaydays – it plays a crucial role in shaping the tenor of the events.

■ Do involve your HR team in the organisation and planning of your awaydays – they are bound to support them, and will appreciate the opportunity to shape what they will regard as very worthwhile events.

Seeking feedback

All of us benefit from feedback about how we are doing in our jobs. A sensible strategy is to encourage feedback rather than wait for it.

Frequency – periodic.
Key participants – colleagues and peers.
Leadership rating ***

Objective

Few of us, if any, actually go to work wanting to do a bad job – it would be perverse, given how much of our waking lives we devote to it. By the same token, if we are honest we also want to know how we are doing – what areas we are strong in, and what areas can be improved. We may be more reluctant – out of embarrassment or fear – to confront the benefits that such feedback provides, and systems often have to be put in place to ensure that such feedback actually occurs.

As a leader you should actively encourage and welcome feedback mechanisms as a powerful tool for improving your own performance. You should understand that feedback is more than annual or semi-annual performance appraisal. It is not just about what your line manager thinks of you in a hierarchical structure. Finally, you should appreciate that a thorough and ongoing approach to feedback is absolutely about improving you and not trying to catch you out.

*Your challenge is to accept feedback as enhancing rather than debilitating – **a support and not a threat to you as an individual**.*

Context

Any feedback structure or process should be viewed as part of a broader approach to people-development (of which you are a part) and is fundamentally based on five human resource principles.

- **Core competencies** – having a clear view of what competencies (or capabilities) your organisation needs to deliver its strategic objectives. These are to be distinguished from those capabilities that can be outsourced and are to be reviewed as part of the annual strategic planning process.

- **Organisation structure** – getting your organisation structured so that your competencies are best aligned to your market needs. This is likely to be reviewed on an almost constant basis.

- **Recruitment and retention** – how you appoint and keep the people you need to maintain your core competency talent pool. This is delivered by constant attention to market salary and benefits standards, and through development opportunity planning.

- **Talent management** – a structured process by which an organisation ensures that its talent pool meets its organisational needs, that development opportunities are planned for and skills gaps identified.

- **Career development** – development planning for each individual, ensuring that they are challenged to reach their full potential.

The opportunity to get feedback from a range of sources (as I describe below) is part of an overall approach to making sure the right people are in the right jobs performing the best they can.

Challenge

The biggest single obstacle to getting the best from constructive feedback will be yourself. The most likely barriers will be:

- **fear** – you don't want to hear what others think about you;

- **scepticism** – while you accept that feedback has its place, you don't really believe that it is likely to lead to any perceptible change in your or others' behaviour or performance;

- **arrogance** – you don't believe that you could benefit from feedback;
- **narrowness of vision** – you don't recognise how wide the range of sources is from whom you might seek feedback;
- **time** – you rank feedback low in your list of priorities, and there is always something more important to do.

Best of all, you need humility to recognise that you can always improve, and that others can always provide insights into how you can achieve this. You also need the support of really excellent HR professionals who can help you through their commitment and processes.

Success

Achieving a successful 'feedback loop' – receiving feedback and acting on it – can be based on three sources.

- **Normal corporate feedback processes**:
  - regular 121s with your boss – ask to be told how they think you are doing and give areas where you can improve;
  - regular 121s with your direct reports – encourage them to feedback how you can enhance their performance through doing more of what you do well, and less of what you do badly;
  - annual performance appraisals – while these often have far more significance than they merit[1], appraisals should provide an opportunity for the participants to stand back and take a medium- to long-term view of performance.
- **Partners** – it is easy forget that you interact with, and therefore your performance and effectiveness are judged by, a very wide range of people outside your employing

---

1 Performance appraisal is a subject in its own right. Annual appraisals frequently assume a far greater significance than they merit because they are the only point in the year when the appraisee receives feedback. If this is the case, then ongoing feedback processes are not working.

organisation. These might include customers, suppliers, business partners (including in joint ventures (JVs)), your financial advisers, industry associations etc. Why not take the opportunity to ask them what they think?

■ **360 degree processes** – '360° feedback' is becoming increasingly popular and is much favoured by HR professionals.

Leaders' measures of success

→ You receive feedback regularly from your line manager.

→ You participate in 360° processes.

→ You ask partners from outside your organisation for their feedback.

Pitfalls

In the end, feedback only works in a constructive virtuous circle – feedback leading to improvement – when the feedback itself is appropriate and directed, and when it is acted on.

■ **Untimely feedback** – it is unwise to put your team members on the spot by asking them to provide feedback about you and your performance if they are unprepared and not ready for it. The embarrassment and difficulty it may cause will outweigh any feedback benefits. It is probably wise to only ask for advice and feedback when the nature of the relationships in your team have developed to the extent that such feedback can be given without any feeling that their relationship with you as line manager is being compromised.

■ **Ignored feedback** – there is clearly no point in asking for feedback if you do nothing about it! This will only compound whatever observations were being made in the feedback itself with the overwhelming perception that you are deaf to criticism and unwilling to change. In this case, it would be better not to ask for feedback at all.

The moral here is that feedback is deeply personal – not only for you but also for the colleagues giving it. Choosing to seek it is a major (positive) step – but you must choose your time carefully and be seen to act on it.

Leaders' checklist

- First and foremost, recognise that feedback plays a vital role in the management, development and improvement of your performance.

- If you feel uncomfortable about receiving feedback, learn to talk with one of your HR team – or someone more 'independent' – to get informal feedback.

- Try to take the opportunity of having 121s with your team members to identify ways you can learn and develop, but handle this sensitively – they may also feel intimidated about criticising you!

- Encourage the use of 360° processes, not simply for yourself but also for your team members – this will help to break down 'feedback barriers'.

ten

Resources: the leadership toolkit

Much of this book is about what leaders need to do –
what actions they should take to position themselves
as leaders, to enable their key staff to become leaders
in their own right, and to make their business units or
organisations leaders in their class. To a very great extent,
success in achieving leadership status depends upon
each leader looking inside him or herself and drawing
upon, or optimising, natural leadership qualities. Great
leaders look outside themselves, and not just at the
immediate colleagues they can develop and who, as
I described earlier in the book (see p. 88), are usually
more skilled than the leader is anyway! What the best
leaders do is draw on any resources available to improve
their effectiveness, and to be unashamed and open in
doing so. This is part of any leader's essential humility –
knowing what they don't know and being prepared to do
something about it!

This final part is a limited attempt to distil some ideas
about three resource areas on which leaders should draw.

- **Human resources** – key areas within what is typically called 'HR' which can assist you in your recruitment, development and management of key staff.

- **Technology resources** – those areas of technological innovation with which any leader must be familiar.

- **Learning resources** – suggested further reading, in book and digital form, for each of the chapters of this book.

As a leader it is vital that you never stop learning, and that you recognise that learning is an endless journey. No amount of experience is ever a reason to cease learning – indeed experience teaches the best leaders that the more they learn the more they realise how little they know.

Human resources

'HR' can all too easily be seen as the department which helps with hiring and firing, with some training in-between. While for some this may be a caricature, it does highlight the important decision leaders must make about how HR contributes to their effectiveness. In essence there is a simple but fundamental choice – as a leader either you involve HR fully and totally in your management and decision-making processes, or you don't. If HR *is* fully involved, then it plays a key part in shaping and implementing your Vision and strategy. If it is *not*, then it is essentially an administrative adjunct on the receiving end of decisions.

My view is that you should put HR at the heart of your leadership style, your thinking and your approaches. Your HR colleagues will help you to be a better and more effective leader because they can help you to think about what leadership means rather than simply implement decisions you make.

This chapter is not intended to give a comprehensive list of activities that HR teams undertake. Rather it is an insight – organised alphabetically for convenience – of those areas you should consider as vital in your role as leader, and why.

Bonuses

Bonuses are a really important of your leadership armoury, despite the bad press associated with them (largely through their use in financial services). Your approach to bonuses should be based on two principles – that staff are paid for above-target performance and not as a matter of right, and that they have an appropriate balance between personal, team and company performance. Your HR team will help you to calibrate this in respect of individuals and also within any norms set by your organisation.

Bullying

There is no organisation at any stage or of any size, nor any management group so senior, in which bullying is acceptable. Defined as *'repeated, health-harming mistreatment, verbal abuse; or conduct which is threatening, humiliating, intimidating; or sabotage that interferes with work – or some combination of the three'* (Workplace Bullying Institute), bullying is insidious and often goes unnoticed. As a leader, you must stand up against any form of bullying whatsoever, and be seen to do so. You must take seriously any complaints about bullying and ensure that your HR investigates such claims thoroughly and promptly.

Coaching

While 'training' often defines a formal at-work learning process with defined (sometimes qualification-related) outcomes, 'coaching' describes a less formal process by which individuals reflect and build on their workplace experience, using the guiding power of someone with greater experience or specific counselling skills. You may find yourself coaching your own staff on a day-to-day basis, but you can – and should – deploy coaching processes for individuals with specific development issues. If you are prepared to commit to it, using the services of external, professional coaches is likely to be the most effective approach.

Culture

If someone in your team is asked what it's like to work in your organisation, their answer will probably describe your organisation's culture. You need to be aware that you will *create* a culture within your team or organisation, whether you choose to knowingly or not – in which case it is advisable to take a 'knowing' approach and think about the culture characteristics you want to achieve. These are likely to be shaped around your approach to people, ideas and performance.

Disciplinary systems

All organisations have disciplinary systems and as a leader you should ensure you are familiar with them, their role and how and when you use them. Above all else be committed to using them, with the guidance of HR, when you need to. They will focus on issues relating to *conduct* – the appropriateness of behaviour; and *performance* – the standard of achievement. The real hallmark of an effective leader is a willingness to confront people-performance issues when they exist, and disciplinary systems are one of a number of tools at your disposal.

Diversity

A corporate approach to 'diversity' is not just about ensuring that you meet all legal workplace obligations relating to, for example, gender, sexuality or disability – that should be a given. It is about an ethical commitment to ensure that your organisation is an appropriate and supportive environment for minority groups, and that the constituency of your employees reflects the diversity and balance of the broader national population. You may not feel especially empowered as an individual to influence the corporate stance on diversity, but you will in any event send many signals about your stance on the issue – driven primarily by who you employ, how you treat them and what you are heard to say about workplace issues.

Feedback

We all need to know how well we are doing at work (or not!) and as a leader you must set the standard in ensuring that feedback is provided regularly, thoroughly and appropriately. This is not about 'appraisal' systems – which are annual or biannual reviews that are more strategic in nature (see below) – but ongoing commentary designed to encourage ever-higher performance. Feedback must not only be characterised as suggestions for improvement, but also as praise for what has gone right so that positive behaviour is reinforced.

Grievance procedures

Circumstances will arise at work where individuals have specific complaints about others. Sometimes these can be mediated and resolved informally; sometimes they are more serious in nature or conviction and have to handled through formal grievance procedures. Your HR team will advise when this is necessary and how the procedures are to be operated. Your challenge, and responsibility, as leader is not the processes – these will be well-established and circumscribed by legal employment obligations. Your role is to ensure that you create a culture in which issues that can become – or are – grievances are aired, discussed and resolved (however painfully). You must not allow or tolerate an environment in which issues are swept under the carpet.

Health issues

It is easy to allow health issues to become less important than work, especially if you are the kind of individual that focuses on performance and separates the professional from the private. But, put very simply, anyone's good health is their most precious asset and as a leader you must always, without question, support anyone in whatever way necessary with health issues that need attention.

Holidays

Taking holidays is an important part of working effectively. All staff need regular breaks to recharge their batteries and to be able to take a fresh perspective on their working lives. There is no merit whatsoever in not taking a full holiday allowance, and you should encourage all your staff to take all their entitlement – and you should be seen to take the lead in doing so yourself.

Incentives

As leader you should want your staff to earn as much as possible, and in particular you should recognise the value that specific incentive programmes bring. This can include a wide range of methods including commission, bonuses, bounty payments and various share plans. The key issue for you as leader is to take a view about the appropriateness of specific incentives to achievement goals and to ensure that they are tailored appropriately. Your HR team should play a key role in assisting with this assessment.

International culture

There are few organisations which don't have an international dimension through some combination of their supplier base, their client pool and their own office and staff locations. Ensuring that staff have appropriate international knowledge and sensitivity is therefore a key requirement for you and your HR team. It will take a wide range of forms depending on your specific business, but might include specific training workshops, recruiting HQ-based staff with a wide range of language skills, transferring staff internationally on work placements, transferring staff internationally on longer-term assignments, and even, where possible, encouraging staff to travel internationally to meet overseas colleagues.

Management structure

Your management structure is a vital part of your leadership toolkit, ensuring that you face your markets with the appropriate, focused competence. This should never be regarded as fixed, and you should always be prepared to adapt your structure to meet new circumstances. Your HR team can help you to think through the ways in which you 'pair' market needs with available internal competence and recruitment possibilities.

Meetings

I have described the importance of bringing staff together, actually or virtually, for regular opportunities to communicate and share information (see the chapter called *Staff meetings*, p. 119). The key elements in this process are to ensure that you are *committed* to such meetings and that they actually take place; to *think through* the way they should be structured – it's about much more than simply getting people in a room or on the phone; and to *provide feedback* on how the meetings are progressing, whether they are working or not and what other staff are saying about them.

Mentoring

Mentors can at certain stages in individuals' careers play a vital role in their personal development. A mentor provides a form of confessional – an environment in which you can discuss, in private, workplace issues and people, and seek advice from someone with greater experience. There is a significant difference between coaching and mentoring – coaching is usually provided by an external professional expert against a specific set of agreed learning outcomes; mentoring is a broader and looser internal opportunity to provide organisation- and experience-based counselling. Your HR team will be able to help you to think through when either of these is an appropriate course of action, and how it should be organised.

Performance appraisal

We are all so well aware of the concept of annual appraisal that it may seem unlikely that there is anything new or insightful that anyone could say about it. But that is precisely the point – assumptions about appraisal are embedded, and your HR team, if it is effective, will challenge you about your appraisal process to ensure that you understand that it is not the sole annual point for feedback, that you regard it is an opportunity for broader strategic reflection, and that you utilise it to discuss career planning and personal development.

Personal development plans

These are a natural offshoot of appraisals and may often lead to potentially expensive or time-consuming suggestions for management training courses up to and including MBAs. The role your HR team can play is threefold – it can help you to think through the appropriate development strategies for each individual; it can assist in prioritisation; and it can creatively think about cost-effective solutions when, inevitably, training and development budgets are always lower than ideal.

Recruitment

The value of recruitment can be overlooked, because it can become a case-by-case *process* rather than a strategic tool. As a leader you should set yourself the goal of establishing, with your HR team, a set of principles to guide all your recruitment to help you to achieve your strategic goals. You should especially ensure that HR is empowered to determine the competence profiles for all key recruits to ensure that you recruit to market needs and not to your own image.

Retention

This is always tough. You can't promote everyone but that doesn't mean you aren't more than satisfied with everyone's performance. You need to work with your HR team to have a clear view of the potential of each key individual and how the combination of personal development plan, specific training opportunity and compensation package will provide them with sufficient incentive and challenge to stay within the organisation.

Salary benchmarking

Salary levels in any organisation can become driven by historical precedent rather than market conditions, and you must ensure with your HR team that where necessary – sometimes at annual review points, sometimes when you are recruiting – you benchmark your salaries against external salary levels. There are software packages and/or organisations than can do this for you.

Salary reviews

Salary reviews are typically undertaken on an annual basis, and it is my view that while this is so for reasons of convenience, budgeting and inflation cycles, you should be clear that such a review is separate from performance – the latter being reflected in incentive and bonus structures. You should also be prepared to work with your HR team to assess salaries whenever it seems appropriate, or whenever staff request a review, provided they understand that the word 'review' is not synonymous with 'increase'. HR teams will help you to ensure that – within company policies governing standard increases, for example – you apply any discretion on a fair and consistent basis.

Talent management

Any business depends on ensuring that it has the right talent – the right people with the right skills in the right jobs – and this requires planning. It demands a clear understanding of the organisation's needs and how these are changing; appropriate external recruitment and internal development; transparent performance management and monitoring; and, above all else, a system that brings all these together. Such a 'talent management' system can be deployed by HR teams to provide a tracking mechanism for key staff to ensure that there are robust processes for succession planning.

Training

Your HR team can add real value in your thinking about training and the place it has in your career development processes. Training can sometimes be categorised or regarded as attending courses, and you should work with your staff to ensure they realise that training is not a checklist process of this kind – and, more importantly, that in-work, on-the-job training can be just as effective as any external event. The key here is to ensure that training opportunities are truly calibrated to individual needs.

Working environment

Don't ever underestimate the extent to which your immediate working environment affects culture and performance. You should consider such questions as: Where is the office located? Can it be reached by public transport? Is it close to shops? Is the office large enough to have its own café/canteen/restaurant? Is the office open-plan or structured around offices and partitions? Is it clean and recently painted? Is it kept tidy? These and many other factors will affect how your colleagues feel about working with you and each other – and for many the way the organisation presents itself through its offices speaks volumes about its values. Your HR team can help you to assess these environmental factors with a dispassionate people-orientated perspective.

Technology resources

There is, of course, little in our business lives which is not touched by technology and it would be foolish to think that any summary in a book of this kind could do full justice to the growing potential of what is available. Nor could I aspire to present the value of technology from the perspective of an IT professional. However, what I do hope this section can do is ensure that the opportunity presented by technology is seen for what it is – all-encompassing for the business leader, and a key instrument of change.

Blackberries

Maybe the bane of personal lives – how many of us have them flashing at our bedsides! – but such devices are a vital tool in modern communication. Together with laptops/netbooks and even the new iPad, their key role is supporting the trend towards mobile living and working. The key here is that it matters less where you work, but that you are connected. What Blackberries should not be is a perk for more senior staff.

Business communications

Technology can enable immediate and low-cost sharing of data. Use Skype, Instant Messaging and WebEx, for example, to enable personalised, rapid and low-cost international communication, and change your way of working to build them into your working life. Ensure that the purchasing of any of these solutions is as centralised as possible to achieve economies of scale.

Call centres

The focus on call centres is frequently around the outsourcing and offshoring issue – where should they be based? This is certainly a key business challenge – given the growth of the international use of English, there are real opportunities to locate call centres in low-cost environments like India and the Philippines. However, given the rise of extensive business process outsourcing (BPO) locations, and given the widespread use of automated and speech recognition-based telephony systems and chat-based interaction, call-centre management is becoming a commodity. The real technology opportunity in call centres lies at the next stage – what data can you collect from customers? And what can you do with it?

Corporate communications

Gone are the days when corporate communications comprised an AGM, an annual report and the occasional press release. Webcasting enables messages to reach many internal and external audiences fully and in real time; websites enable far more information to be released and in flexible formats. But the most powerful change is that technology enables corporate communications to move from *broadcast* to *interactive* mode – businesses no longer tell customers what they think, but businesses and customers share views together.

Corporate governance

Corporate governance can seem remote to many staff, but there are multiple ways in which organisations need to comply – legal, financial and regulatory. An organisation may also set its own value standards, which it wishes staff to follow. Compliance always requires a trail of credible information, and technology should be used to create auditable processes and responses.

Corporate social networking

It is frequently a challenge in organisations (especially large and multi-national ones) to keep tabs on who is who and who is doing what. Traditional information-sharing mechanisms – organisation charts, cross-company meetings etc. – are often out of date and infrequent. So the transparency and rapidity of information and its sharing, which we have all been used to in the private-life world of *Facebook* and *MySpace*, should be brought into the workplace. Tools like *Yammer* enable what can be called 'enterprise micro-blogging' through which like-minded individuals create and share a virtual network of common competence, interest and intelligence. All business leaders should encourage, use and draw from this kind of system – find out what colleagues know and what they really think!

Customer services

It is too easy to think of customer services as being represented by scripted call agents answering queries in a (possibly offshore) call centre. Certainly this is an (increasingly sophisticated) aspect of providing excellent service. But the power of technology can transform such services from being organisation- or supplier-centred (with inbound queries answered against a list of frequently asked questions) to being customer-centred. This means using data gathered about the purchasing habits of customers to provide an increasingly proactive rather than reactive approach. It means regarding 'service' as a tool to generate loyalty and future sales rather than a defence against failure.

Digital marketing

The core of your digital marketing will be your websites, and the key challenge here is to ensure that you don't regard it as a static billboard. It will power a deep range of activities – product marketing; product demos, e-commerce, customer communities, corporate information and feedback loops. Maximising its potential demands two key attitudinal shifts – that you bring into your organisation the perspective of 'digital natives' so that you understand all media and communication possibilities; and that you continuously review and refresh your approach – even when it is appropriate, it will age rapidly.

Inventory management and fulfilment

The key issue with inventory is always cash. All goods unsold (wherever they are in the supply chain) represent cash not working! So regard inventory systems less about measuring what stock you have, and more about limiting what stock you have (through the closest 'just-in-time' systems with suppliers and customers) and also knowing where it is (if you can measure it, you can control it!). Also use measurement systems which track stock to provide better service delivery systems to customers.

Manufacturing

No note of this kind could begin to do justice to the application of technology to manufacturing. The point to make here is that the rapid growth of manufacturing centres (notably China), coupled with a huge growth in all levels of education and investment in both R&D and academic research, is contributing to the emergence of wholly new global centres of manufacturing excellence. This is expanding the range of manufacturing choices for all purchasers with significant benefits – lower cost, reduced supply chains and improved design. So if you have any kind of responsibility for engineering or manufacturing, make no assumptions about what can be made where!

Market research and surveys

Gone are the days of surveys undertaken by researchers carrying clipboards on the high street. Gone too are postal surveys. Backed by increasingly sophisticated customer relationship management (CRM) database systems, surveys for market research are being increasingly automated to ever more focused niche customer groups. And these can be very cost-effective – see *www.survey-monkey.com*.

Payroll and benefits

There is nothing new about being paid electronically. But until recently, payment advice was paper-based, as was much information about related benefits (sickness, incentives, savings plans). Now providers can spend all this data electronically, and you should regard this as an opportunity to reduce transaction costs and improve service to employees – in one place employees can access data on pay, benefits and incentives, for example.

Procurement

Traditional procurement (purchasing) markets are notoriously inefficient, primarily because of a lack of awareness by purchasers of potential suppliers. The power of the internet, by contrast, enables a much wider exchange of opportunity and identification of possible supplier–partner relationships. At its most sophisticated, for example, it enables routine purchasing to be conducted in real time using online auction processes, whereby competing suppliers bid for contracts (sometimes referred to as 'reverse auctions').

Recruitment

The earliest days of internet innovation brought with them a plethora of sites devoted to recruitment – largely billboards of job ads apparently capable of being matched to your personal preferences. And while this has certainly increased the transparency of vacancies, it is unclear if it has created better matching of job to candidate. For large organisations in particular there is a big gain to be had in implementing web-based e-recruitment systems which apply standard procedures internationally, provide external data links to key recruitment partners and interface with in-company back-office systems.

SEO

Search engine optimisation is a growing discipline at the centre of website management. It has a simple goal – to ensure that your site achieves the highest possible ranking when a relevant web search is made. The challenge for you as a business leader is to ensure that this is *not* seen as a discipline for the marketing department only. This is so fundamental that its role and principles need to be widely understood.

Social media

Corporates increasingly regard sites like *Facebook*, *Twitter* and *MySpace* as a key element of their marketing strategies. This is more than just appearing 'cool' (although this is an element) – it is about creating new ways of engaging with customers and stakeholders, and new ways of gathering market intelligence and feedback. Alongside *YouTube* and your SEO strategy, you should regard maximising the benefits of social media as a fundamental skill set you must develop.

Systems integration

This is possibly the biggest challenge of all. Systems are all too frequently specified and purchased by the functional unit that is going to use them. This leads to both data fragmentation and support/maintenance requirements for a multiplicity of systems. As I mention in *Workflow* below, you need to challenge your organisation to be data-centred and plan systems around that, rather than being function-centred with data trapped in silos. This is a huge challenge to mindsets, procurement and ways of working, but successfully implemented it can achieve real improvements in cost and service.

Talent management

Appraisal systems can be a nightmare of paperwork, and at the very least you should be thinking about how objectives, appraisals and employee information are linked electronically. As you grow – or if you already work in a large organisation – you need systems that enable you to track strengths and weaknesses across large numbers of people to enable, above all else, succession planning.

Telecommunications

It sounds obvious, but you should pool as much data and voice management with as few suppliers as possible. Once data networks are established, the marginal cost to suppliers of providing network minutes is close to zero, and bundling all your requirements will enable significant economies of scale – especially as key providers become increasingly internationalised.

Video

Video is making a comeback. It is undeniably the case that the success of *YouTube* has demonstrated that there is a film-maker or news-reporter in all of us, and that moving-image communication has lost none of its power. The technology is not new, but video plus social media has democratised communication and it has become an increasingly powerful tool for corporates to engage customers and partners. Video is especially powerful for gathering customer testimonials.

Virtual trade fairs

Industry events or trade fairs are well established, and many are a major fixed point in organisation calendars. But they are an expensive and logistically demanding way of interacting with partners and customers. Increasingly you will find businesses interacting with customers via online fairs, where virtual reality software and social media combine to create a virtual 'exchange'. These are potentially extremely attractive when customers are very broadly spread geographically.

Websites

It goes without saying that every business has a website – they are a commodity. But as a leader you have a choice – do you want a billboard or do you want a living, breathing organism? Do you want to broadcast or do you want to interact? Do you want to tell or also listen? Do you want to be closed or open? See your website as the world's window on you, not your window on the world. Use each and every technology – social media, video, communities, e-commerce, instant messaging – to create multiple access points where customers draw you into their world.

Workflow

In most functions or teams, work consists of a series of connected processes. Excellent businesses are already adept at knowing how to simplify and manage these interactions, including with external partners. But since most interactions are based on the sharing and movement of data, often between different execution platforms, far more radical changes are possible. Consider, then, implementing workflow management systems which are data- rather than function-centred. This will actually force you to rethink the processes you had in place which you believed were excellent, but which were actually based around management rather than data structures.

Learning resources

By definition, we learn while we are working. Experience is in many ways the best tutor when you are a business leader. But it always repays the effort – even if time seems to be at a premium – to take the advice of other practitioners and experts, which is increasingly available thanks to the diversity of the internet and the relentless growth of international business publishers.

One of the challenges, indeed, is the very scale of the material that is available, and any attempt to provide a comprehensive summary or synopsis of the best material available would be a project in its own right.

So what I have attempted to do here is to a provide some directions, chapter by chapter, to print- or web-based documents which you might want to consider as useful reference material. It has worked for me, and may do so for you. Remember that it is intended to be a pointer – not a detailed bibliography or survey – so take it for what it is.

Part one: Your leadership self

First days in the job

- The most widely-cited book relating to this area is *The First 90 Days: Critical Success Strategies for New Leaders at All Levels* by Michael Watkins (Harvard Business School Press, 2003). My time frame is much shorter, and I think that the focus on an initial 90- or 100-day period can underestimate the lasting impact of first encounters.
- I like what I see in *Projects@Work*, a website dedicated to project management tools. www.projectsatwork.com/content/articles/247953.cfm is an article which highlights the importance of first days.

Demeanour: setting the tone

- For the impact of demeanour, read any review (and there are many) of the initial period of the Obama presidency and its differences from the Bush era. See for example *Time*, April 23, 2009 – 'Perhaps Obama's most dramatic departure from the recent past is his public presence: cool where George W. Bush seemed hot; fluent where Bush seemed tongue-tied; palliative rather than hortative' (Joe Klein).

Leadership principles

- If you are interested in reading an example of a major international organisation committing itself to leadership principles publicly, then see Nestlé at www.nestle.com.
- See also *Leadership Principles: The Basis of Successful Leadership* by Russell E. Palmer (Wharton School Publishing, 2008).

Trusting your instincts

- http://www.bizjournals.com/charlotte/stories/2004/11/01/smallb4.html offers a provoking article relating instinct and intuition to so-called 'artful' leadership. You will first need to sign up to an excellent service called BNET – http://bnet.co.uk
- See also *The DNA of Leadership: Leverage Your Instincts to Communicate, Differentiate, Innovate* by Judith E. Glaser (Platinum Press, 2006).

Focusing on what matters

- See www.thepracticeofleadership.net/2009/04/13/keeping-your-leadership-focus/ for guidance on focus. More generally, *The practice of leadership* site is, I have found, a very good source of summary practical advice.

Managing meetings

- For a lively approach to managing meetings see www. businessballs.com (and for much more besides!).

- Amazon lists 2196 books at the time of writing under the subject 'managing meetings', a subject I have never really thought merited book-length treatment. The long-established *How to Hold Successful Meetings: 30 Action Tips for Managing Effective Meetings* by Paul Timm (Career Press, 1990) has at least the advantage of brevity (it is part of the *30-Minute Solution Series*).

Time management

- The sheer plurality of material available on time management (> 18500 entries on Amazon) indicates how this is an enduring and vexing subject. I remain concerned that books tend to overcomplicate a subject requiring simplification.

- See www.time-management-guide.com and www. businessballs.com for some short and to-the-point guidance.

- The *YouTube* video 'Time management' by Randy Pausch (November, 2007) is an entertaining and accessible challenge.

You and your boss

- For an amusing description of the different types of boss you will face (from 'toxic shit' to 'saint') see Stefan Stern on 'How to manage your boss' in *Management Today* at www.managementtoday.co.uk/search/article/452965/ how-manage-boss/

- See also *How to Manage Your Boss* by Ros Jay (Prentice Hall, 2002).

Part two: Vision and strategy: the leadership mantra

Setting and selling a Vision

- See *Harvard Business Review on Leadership* (HBR, 1997) pp 40–50 and 86. This remains a popular and much-reprinted classic.

Leading strategy

- So much is written on strategy that highlighting specific resources is extremely risky. *Competitive Strategy* by Michael E. Porter (Free Press, 2004) should be on any manager's bookshelf. For a current Google-esque world view to challenge your assumptions see *What Would Google Do?* by Jeff Davis (Harper Collins, 2009).

- Your organisation can consider many strategy tools – the Boston Consulting Group's 'Product Portfolio Matrix' and the Harvard 'Balanced Scorecard' are two such examples.

International markets and strategy

- A sound foundation is provided by *Global Strategic Management* 2nd edition by Philippe Lasserre (Palgrave Macmillan, 2007) and *International Business: Strategy, Management and the New Realities* by Tamer Cavusgil, Gary Knight and John Riesenberger (Prentice Hall, 2008).

- Almost any issue of the *Harvard Business Review* will provide insights to shape your international perspective.

Leadership priorities

- *The Art and Discipline of Strategic Leadership* by Mike Freedman (Kepner-Tregoe, 2003) is a powerful description of the relentless and disciplined approach required for successful strategy implementation.

Part three: Your leadership team

Defining your leadership team

- See *Management Teams: Why They Succeed or Fail* 2nd edition by R. Meredith Belbin (Elsevier Butterworth Heinemann, 2003).

Managing your leadership team

- See *Overcoming the Five Dysfunctions of a Team: A Field Guide for Leaders, Managers and Facilitators* by Patrick M. Lencioni (Jossey Bass, 2005).
- Excellent and practical resources are available at www.businessballs.com
- If you are interested in learning more about 'Forming–Storming–Norming–Performing' see 'Developmental sequence in small groups', *Psychological Bulletin* 63 (6): 384–99 by Bruce Tuckman.

121s

- For a detailed discussion of performance management strategies see *Performance Management: Key Strategies and Practical Guidelines* 3rd edition by Michael Armstrong (Kogan Page, 2006).
- http://en.wordpress.com/tag/121s/ contains some interesting conversations about the effectiveness of 121s.

Your team is more skilled than you

- *The Leader's Guide to Lateral Thinking Skills: Unlocking the Creativity and Innovation in You and Your Team* 2nd edition by Paul Sloane (Kogan Page, 2004) describes a range of techniques you can employ to optimise the contribution each of your team members can make.

Team members in other countries

- For specific guidance on employment practices by jurisdiction, your organisation is best advised to use the service of HR specialists such as Watson Wyatt.

- There are many web-based services that claim to offer comparisons of salaries worldwide, though the data is unlikely to be up-to-date given major changes in economic circumstances and exchange rates. *The Economist* publishes a useful annual cost of living index (see www.economist.com).

Part four: Leading your organisation

Credibility from repetition

- A useful resource across many areas of this book is *How to Lead: What You Actually Need to Do to Manage, Lead and Succeed* 2nd edition by Jo Owen (Pearson Education, 2009). It has a humanistic core that puts people at the centre of the leadership endeavour.

Resistance to change

- *Who Moved My Cheese? An Amazing Way to Deal with Change in Your Work and in Your Life* by Spencer Johnson (Vermilion, 1999) remains a popular work on changing assumptions, starting with yourself.

- www.businessballs.com has an excellent section on the subject of change, with some amusing ideas relating to the use of Aesop's fables.

Process: making the right things happen at the right time

- Much has been written about process as it relates to process-intensive (often engineering or manufacturing) activities. See for example *The Lean Six Sigma Pocket Toolbook* by Michael L. George, John Maxey, David T. Rowlands and Malcolm Upton

(McGraw Hill, 2005). Much less is written about embedding process in our approach to all activities and as a leadership mantra.

Staff meetings

■ See BNET for a range of articles on meetings – e.g. 'How to run an Effective Staff Meeting'.

Collaborating with sister businesses

■ There seems to have been relatively little written on this subject. *The Six Dilemmas of Collaboration: Inter-organisational Relationships as Drama* by Jim Bryant (John Wiley, 2003) sees inter-divisional partnering in terms of drama, which may not be to everyone's taste.

Part five: Leading performance excellence

Managing change

■ One of my favourite books on this subject remains *My Iceberg is Melting* by John Kotter (Macmillan, 2006).

■ *Who Moved My Cheese ? An Amazing Way to Deal with Change in Your Work and in Your Life* by Spencer Johnson (Vermilion, 1999) remains a classic for its adept yet striking simplicity, and for portraying so keenly how personal change can feel.

People performance management

■ A really detailed description of the many-layered stages of performance and improvement management is provided by Michael Armstrong in *Performance Management: Key Strategies and Practical Guidelines* 3rd edition (Kogan Page, 2006).

■ The Chartered Institute of Personnel and Development (CIPD), while it is primarily targeted at HR professionals, provides some excellent guidelines well-worth reviewing – see www.cipd.co.uk

Interpersonal conflict

- A popular textbook on the subject remains *Interpersonal Conflict* by William Wilmot and Joyce Hocker (McGraw Hill, 2005).
- The UK conciliation service ACAS has an excellent free booklet about interpersonal conflict called *Managing Conflict at Work* available online at www.acas.org.uk

The difficult interview

- *Managing Difficult People* (HBS Press, 2009) provides some case studies about the challenges of interpersonal relationships.

Objectives and incentives

- Much is written on incentives from either a specific technical or an HR perspective. For managers, there is rather less. *Innovation and Incentives* by S. Scotchmer (MIT Press, 2005) is focused specifically on how incentives need to be structured to drive entrepreneurship, but the principle that incentives need to reflect goals is more widely applicable.
- For objective-setting, see *Setting Goals* in the *Pocket Mentor* series (HBS Press, 2010).
- The blog at www.thepracticeofleadership.net also contains some useful discussions on objectives.

Part six: Customers: leading you

The importance of the customer

- A very old but still excellent training video called *Who Killed the Customer?* remains a powerful resource to show to groups to demonstrate what happens when companies lose sight of the customer.

- An evangelical guide is *Customer is King: How to Exceed Their Expectations* by Sir Richard Branson and Robert Craven (Virgin Books, 2005).

The customer journey 1: customer experience

- *Building Great Customer Experiences* by Colin Shaw and John Ivens (Palgrave Macmillan, 2002) is an exponent of the view I have presented (see especially Chapter 4).
- www.mindtools.com provides an excellent newsletter covering many topics related to interactions with customers.

The customer journey 2: technology journey

- Much is written about using technology to develop customer loyalty, for example *Technology and Customer Service: Profitable Relationship Building* by Paul Timm and Christopher Jones (Prentice Hall, 2004). I find it harder to identify resources which, in a structured manner, describe a process of reviewing all customer technology interfaces.

Sell! Sell! Sell!

- The Institute of Sales and Marketing Management (ISMM) has excellent resources related to strategies and tactics for sales management – see www.ismm.co.uk
- A Muppets training video called *Sell! Sell! Sell!* can be used to energise all staff for sales campaigns.
- The rightly famous *The 7 Habits of Highly Effective People: Personal Workbook* by Stephen R. Covey (Simon and Schuster, 2004) provides some insights into how you should steel yourself to lead attitudinal change.

Part seven: Marketing: leading the market

Marketing is everyone

- The most famous book relating to marketing in its broadest sense is, of course, *The Principles of Marketing* by Philip Kotler (FT Prentice Hall), now in its thirteenth edition and multiple international variants.

- For a more modern and up-to-date view of the rapidly changing world of marketing, try *The New Rules of Marketing and PR: How to Use News Releases, Blogs, Podcasting, Viral Marketing and Online Media to Reach Buyers Direct* by David Meerman Scott (John Wiley, 2008).

- The Chartered Institute of Marketing claims to be the largest professional body worldwide for marketing professionals, and its website at www.cim.co.uk provides access to a wide range of marketing learning and support materials.

Branding and organisational identity

- Three excellent books are:
  - *B2B Brand Management* by Philip Kotler and Waldemar Pfoertsch (Springer, 2006);
  - *Luxury Brand Management* by Michael Chevalier and Gerlad Mazzalovo (John Wiley and Sons, 2008);
  - *The New Strategic Brand Management* 4th edition by Jean Noel Kapferer (Kogan Page, 2008).
- See also the website of the global advertising and marketing agency WPP for a collection of materials about branding in its so-called 'Reading room' – www.wpp.com/wpp/marketing/branding/

Leading product development

- A well-established reference on this subject is *Innovation Management and New Product Development* 4th edition by Paul Trott (FT Prentice Hall, 2008).

- The Product Development and Management Association has some excellent resources at www.pdma.org

Internet transformations

- The video resource referred to in this chapter ('Shift happens: Education 3.0') can be found at www.youtube.com/user/campusvue
- Among many books on this area, consider *Born Digital: Understanding the First Generation of Digital Natives* by John Palfrey and Urs Gasser (Basic Books, 2008).

Part eight: Suppliers and partners: leading together

Building relationships

- There seems to me to be relatively little written specifically in this area, but you might want to try *Managing Business Relationships* by David Ford, LarsErik Gadde, Håkan Håkansson and Ivan Snehota (John Wiley, 2003).
- A very much more recent publication is *Business Relationships that Last: Five Steps that Transform Contacts into High Performing Relationships* by Ed Wallace (Greenleaf Publishing, 2009). What I like about this is that it focuses on the importance of the individual and integrity.

Supplier strategies

- This is a much-published area, with many books focused on the SAP and CRM aspects of managing supplier strategies. For a relationship-orientated view, you could consider *Balanced Sourcing: Cooperation and Competition in Supplier Relationships* (JB BAH Strategy and Business Series) by Timothy M. Laseter (Jossey Bass, 2008).
- An interesting perspective is provided by *The Power of Two: How Smart Companies Create Win:Win Customer–Supplier Partnerships that Outperform the Competition* by C. Cordon

(Palgrave Macmillan, 2008). The central thesis is that organisations benefit from having both fewer suppliers and fewer customers, with a greater focus on both.

Managing costs

- There is a huge amount of information published about the principles and details of cost management from an accounting perspective. I would rather leave this for accountants. More important for organisation leaders is their strategic approach to thinking about cost, and for this you might want to consider *EasyJet: The Story of Britain's Largest Low-cost Airline* by Lois Jones (Aurum Press, 2007).

- If you want a really technical read, try *Cost and Management Accounting* 7th edition by Colin Drury (Cengage Learning, 2007). This is one of the standards of its kind.

Part nine: Learning: leadership development

The knowledge premium

- I think this is a difficult subject to encapsulate. However, try looking at *Working Knowledge: How Organizations Manage What They Know* 2nd edition by Thomas H. Davenport and Laurence Prusak (Harvard University Press, 2000).

- A more recent relevant publication is *Knowledge at Work: Creative Collaboration in the Global Economy* by Robert Defillippi, Michael Arthur and Valerie Lindsay (Wiley–Blackwell, 2006).

Awaydays

- There is a really excellent, though huge, reference on this subject called *Retreats that Work: Everything You Need to Know About Planning and Leading Great Offsites* by Merianne Liteman, Sheila Campbell and Jeffrey Liteman (Jossey Bass, 2006). It is a formidable resource for possible activities during awaydays.

Seeking feedback

- Seeing feedback in the context of an overall approach to coaching is reflected in *The Coaching Manual: The Definitive Guide to the Process, Principles and Skills of Personal Coaching* by Julie Starr (Prentice Hall, 2007).

- www.businessballs.com provides a very broad range of advice on appraisal and feedback, including some sample templates that can be used in specific circumstances.

Index